MORE Greek and Latin Roots

Teaching Vocabulary to Improve Reading Comprehension

Written by
Trisha Callella

Editor: Stacey Faulkner
Illustrator: Corbin Hillam
Cover Designer: Carlie Hayashi
Designer/Production: Cari Helstrom
Art Director: Moonhee Pak
Project Director: Sue Lewis

Table of Contents

Greek and Latin Roots

Introduction

Many students are good decoders—they know how to read a word by sounding out its parts. But often their comprehension of the word's meaning is not as strong. Vocabulary knowledge is an important part of reading comprehension. Research has shown that actively involving students in learning word meanings improves students' comprehension. In fact, improved vocabulary strengthens all areas of literacy—listening, speaking, reading, and writing.

Since increasing and developing students' vocabulary will improve their overall literacy skills and reading comprehension, research recommends teaching students the parts of words. Over 60 percent of all English words have Greek or Latin roots. They are the chunks that contain the essential core meaning of the words students read. Too often, students skip words they do not know as they are reading. This reduces their understanding of the text. For this reason, students need to learn how to break down the meaningful parts of unknown words. As early as second grade, some state writing standards require that students begin to use their knowledge of roots, prefixes, and suffixes to determine the meanings of words. *More Greek and Latin Roots* follows the same easy-to-use format as *Greek and Latin Roots,* and introduces students to 30 new roots and their meanings to support their growing vocabulary.

Use the activities in *More Greek and Latin Roots* to teach your students how to "dissect" and comprehend multisyllabic words, not just decode them. The activities in this resource incorporate all areas of literacy to maximize the transfer of vocabulary into your students' oral language, writing, reading, and comprehension.

Each lesson has four activity pages to teach students new vocabulary:

- A take-home **Word List** that includes the part of speech and definition

- A set of hands-on **Vocabulary Sort** cards students can use to match words and definitions for independent practice

- A set of **Read-Around Review** game cards for small-group interaction, review, and application

- A **Vocabulary Quiz** with multiple choice and fill-in-the blank formats to assess and extend students' learning

Getting Started

Planning and Scheduling

Repetition and review are important factors when learning something new. Incorporate ongoing review activities and games into your everyday curriculum to support vocabulary learning. Ideally, your students will over-learn these roots, so that they become second nature to them. As students become comfortable with "dissecting" and defining word parts, their ability to understand and use larger words will increase. Watch for students to start using the vocabulary you teach in their speech and in their writing!

Adopt the motto "New, New, Review" in your classroom. Because this motto is key to the success of building vocabulary that will transfer to all areas of literacy, *More Greek and Latin Roots* has been designed to support this structure. After every two Greek and/or Latin root lessons, there is a review test. This serves as an easy reminder that ongoing review opportunities are critical to the transfer of learning.

Teach one root each week. This will lead to a three-week teaching cycle. For example, you would teach a new root week 1, a new root week 2, and review the two roots during week 3. The review tests included in the book for each pair of roots will make this schedule easy to follow. Read the information on pages 5 and 6 for directions on how to implement each activity. Use the following Suggested Weekly Plan to help you organize and guide your teaching of Greek and Latin roots and new vocabulary.

 Suggested Weekly Plan

Day 1: **Introduce vocabulary** in a pocket chart.
Play a **game** with the new words (see page 6).
Pass out **Word Lists** to students.

Day 2: **Review vocabulary** in the pocket chart.
Play a **game** with the vocabulary words (see page 6).
Play **Vocabulary Sort**.

Day 3: **Review vocabulary** in the pocket chart.
Use the **Read-Around Review** game cards with small groups.

Day 4: **Review vocabulary** in the pocket chart.
Play a **game** with the vocabulary words (see page 6).
Optional: Have **students make up questions** they think will be on the vocabulary quiz.

Day 5: **Review vocabulary** in the pocket chart.
Have students take the **Vocabulary Quiz**.

Teaching a Lesson

Word List (Days 1–5)

Each lesson begins with a list of ten vocabulary words containing the Greek or Latin root that is the focus for the lesson. The part of speech and the definition are included for each word. Make two copies of the word list for each student. Have students keep one copy at school and take the second copy home so that they can practice learning the words with their families. Follow the steps below to introduce each set of vocabulary words.

- Type each word in a large font. Print and mount the words on a piece of 12" × 18" (30.5 × 46 cm) construction paper—four words to a sheet. Do the same for each definition. Cut apart words and definitions to create individual cards.
- Display only the words in the pocket chart. Read each word and have students repeat it so their pronunciation is correct. After students have had the opportunity to pronounce the words correctly several times, invite them to write the words on the board or in a notebook with the correct syllable breaks.
- Read one definition at a time so that students can apply logic and deduction to figure out which word it defines. Place the correct definition next to the word.
- Display these enlarged word cards in a pocket chart for hands-on manipulation and practice throughout the week. At the end of each week, place the cards together on a ring and neatly store them in a hanging shoe organizer that has clear pockets. Invite students to play games with the cards independently or with partners. This will be a valuable resource during the review week in your teaching cycle.

Vocabulary Sort (Day 2)

Following the Word List of root words and definitions is a list of the same ten words and definitions mixed up and arranged in their own cut-apart slips of paper. This activity is intended to provide hands-on practice with the words.

- Copy a class set of Vocabulary Sort cards on card stock. Have students carefully cut apart the words and definitions, place them in a mailing envelope, and label the envelope with the Greek or Latin root. Have students independently match the words and definitions. Ask them to check their work by referring to their Word List.

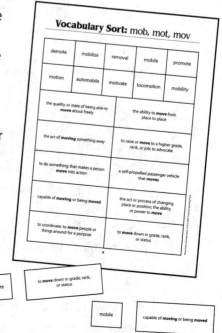

- Give each student a large manila envelope to store his or her individual Vocabulary Sort card envelopes. Have students add sets of cards to this collection all year long. Invite students to use their sets of Vocabulary Sort cards during weeks you are preparing for review tests. This will give students the opportunity to match all of the words and definitions they have learned. This review will challenge students to strengthen their vocabulary as they use words learned in previous lessons.

5

Read-Around Review (Day 3)

This set of cut-apart cards includes the word definitions for all ten words presented in a practical context. Many of the definitions have been reworded to encourage students to think and apply what they have learned about the meanings of words. Use these cards to play an interactive game with your students.

- Copy a set of cards on card stock for each small group of three or four students. Cut apart the cards and laminate them. Place each set of cards in an envelope and write the heading *Read-Around Review* at the top. Label the envelope with the matching Greek or Latin root (e.g., *mob, mot, mov*).

- Give each group a set of cards. Ask students to divide the cards equally among the group members. Have students silently read their cards several times. Discuss any questions students have before beginning the game. Tell the group that the student who has the clue card that says *I have the first card* will begin the game by reading aloud his or her card. The student whose card has the answer to the clue should read aloud his or her card. Tell students to continue until all cards have been read.

Games (Days 1, 2, 4)

- **VOCABO:** Give each student a blank piece of paper. Have students draw three lines across and three lines down to make a 4 × 4 grid similar to a tic-tac-toe board. Tell them to write the vocabulary words and roots in any boxes they want as you say the words. Have students designate one box as a "free space." After students' boards are filled in, play as you would play BINGO by reading a definition and having students mark the matching vocabulary word or root on their board.

- **What's the Secret Word?:** Divide the class into two groups. Choose two "contestants" to stand in front of each group. Reveal a secret word to each group. Have contestants take turns calling on volunteers to share one-word clues to help them guess the secret word. Students' clues will build on one another to narrow down the choices. For an extra challenge, set a time limit. The contestant to guess the word remains at the front of the group, and the student who gave the final clue replaces the other contestant. Repeat play with a new word.

- **Vocabulary Baseball:** Divide the class into two mixed-ability teams and designate four places in the room as "bases." Have each batter decide if he or she wants to attempt a single, double, triple, or home run, and then have the opposing team choose a word. To hit a single, the batter tells the definition of the word. To hit a double, the batter tells the definition and the part of speech. To hit a triple, the batter tells the root and its meaning. To hit a home run, the batter tells the definition, part of speech, and uses the word correctly in a sentence. All students get a turn before teams switch places.

Assessment (Day 5)

- **Vocabulary Quiz:** Use the 15-question quiz at the end of each lesson to assess students' learning. The quizzes include multiple choice and fill-in-the-blank questions to help prepare students for standardized tests.

- **Review Test:** A 15-question review test follows every two lessons. Each test assesses students' knowledge using a fill-in-the-blank format.

Word List: mob, mot, mov = move

Vocabulary	Definitions
automobile (n)	a self-propelled passenger vehicle that **moves**
demote (v)	to **move** down in grade, rank, or status
locomotion (n)	the ability to **move** from place to place
mobile (adj)	capable of **moving** or being **moved**
mobility (n)	the quality or state of being able to **move** about freely
mobilize (v)	to coordinate; to **move** people or things around for a purpose
motion (n)	the act or process of changing place or position; the ability or power to **move**
motivate (v)	to do something that makes a person **move** into action
promote (v)	to raise or **move** to a higher grade, rank, or job; to advocate
removal (n)	the act of **moving** something away

Vocabulary Sort: mob, mot, mov

demote	mobilize	removal	mobile	promote
motion	automobile	motivate	locomotion	mobility

the quality or state of being able to **move** about freely	the ability to **move** from place to place
the act of **moving** something away	to raise or **move** to a higher grade, rank, or job; to advocate
to do something that makes a person **move** into action	a self-propelled passenger vehicle that **moves**
capable of **moving** or being **moved**	the act or process of changing place or position; the ability or power to **move**
to coordinate; to **move** people or things around for a purpose	to **move** down in grade, rank, or status

8

More Greek and Latin Roots • 4–8 © 2007 Creative Teaching Press

Read-Around Review: mob, mot, mov

I have the first card.

Who has the roots that mean **move**?

I have the word **mobility**.

Who has the word that means the act of **moving** something away from other things, such as taking the trash out of the house?

I have the roots **mob**, **mot**, **mov**.

Who has the word that means a person is **moved** down in his or her rank or status at a job, usually as a result of poor performance?

I have the word **removal**.

Who has the word that describes anything that can be **moved** from place to place?

I have the word **demote**.

Who has the word that means the simple act of **movement**?

I have the word **mobile**.

Who has the word that means a vehicle that **moves** people around town?

I have the word **motion**.

Who has the word that means the ability of the human body to **move** from place to place?

I have the word **automobile**.

Who has the word that names what you might do if you try to get a group of people organized to support a special cause?

I have the word **locomotion**.

Who has the word that means to **move** up in a person's job status or rank, usually due to excellent performance and work ethics?

I have the word **mobilize**.

Who has the word that means to do something that makes a person want to **move** into action?

I have the word **promote**.

Who has the word that means the quality or state of being able to **move** about freely?

I have the word **motivate**.

Who has the first card?

More Greek and Latin Roots • 4–8 © 2007 Creative Teaching Press

Name _____   Date _____

Vocabulary Quiz: mob, mot, mov

Shade in the bubble for the correct word.

1. Keith was having a hard time getting excited about going to the gym. "What does he need?"
   Ⓐ **mobility**   Ⓑ **motivation**   Ⓒ **motion**   Ⓓ **promotion**

2. What are simple movements such as raising or clapping your hands called?
   Ⓐ **motions**   Ⓑ **promotions**   Ⓒ **demotions**   Ⓓ **motivation**

3. Which word below describes a cell phone or MP3 player?
   Ⓐ **mobile**   Ⓑ **mobility**   Ⓒ **demotion**   Ⓓ **automobile**

4. Mr. Wilcox was late to work on too many days so his boss considered doing *this* to him.
   Ⓐ **mobilizing**   Ⓑ **promoting**   Ⓒ **motivating**   Ⓓ **demoting**

5. Ashley was planning to get all of her friends to join her in the protest. "What does she need to do to her friends?"
   Ⓐ **demote**   Ⓑ **promote**   Ⓒ **mobilize**   Ⓓ **remove**

6. Lucas purchased a new hybrid car that gets the best mileage of any car in its class. "What did Lucas purchase?"
   Ⓐ **automobile**   Ⓑ **motivation**   Ⓒ **mobility**   Ⓓ **motion**

7. After Linda broke her leg, she lay in bed with her leg in a sling for three weeks. "What did she not have?"
   Ⓐ **motivation**   Ⓑ **demotions**   Ⓒ **automobile**   Ⓓ **mobility**

8. When you finish the school year with outstanding grades you will be moved to the next grade. "Which word below describes what will happen to you?"
   Ⓐ **promoted**   Ⓑ **motivated**   Ⓒ **mobilized**   Ⓓ **demoted**

9. It was painful when the dentist took out Nick's back molar. "What did the dentist do to the molar?"
   Ⓐ **motivated**   Ⓑ **demoted**   Ⓒ **promoted**   Ⓓ **removed**

10. People who have Parkinson's disease may develop problems with which ability?
    Ⓐ **demotion**   Ⓑ **promotion**   Ⓒ **locomotion**   Ⓓ **removal**

Write the correct word on the line so that the sentence makes sense and sounds grammatically correct.

11. Leslie was given two _____ due to her hard work and dedication to the company.

12. Sarah announced her plans to _____ the participants for the rally.

13. Self-_____ helps students be more successful than being rewarded with money or items for good grades.

14. The disruptive student was _____ from the classroom.

15. Workers with bad attitudes are often _____, so they make less money and have less important positions.

More Greek and Latin Roots • 4–8 © 2007 Creative Teaching Press

Word List: grad, gress = step

Vocabulary	Definitions
aggressive (adj)	hostile; pushy; **stepping** into someone's space with forceful energy
centigrade (adj)	Celsius; temperature rating on the thermometer made up of 100 degree intervals or **steps** between the freezing and boiling points of water
degrade (v)	to reduce someone's worth or value; to make someone **step** down to a lower position or rank; to move down a **step** in social status
digress (v)	to stray away from the main topic; to **step** away from the topic and lose clarity; to wander in thoughts or ideas
gradual (adj)	a slow change; a **step-by-step** change
graduate (v)	to move up a **step** in education (usually out of a school)
progress (v)	to move a **step** in a positive direction; to improve; to move a **step** closer to a goal
progression (n)	a **step-by-step** sequence within a continuous series
regress (v)	to go back; to move backward; to move a **step** back
upgrade (v)	to move up a **step** or level; to improve in quality

More Greek and Latin Roots • 4–8 © 2007 Creative Teaching Press

Vocabulary Sort: grad, gress

regress	digress	progress	upgrade	degrade
graduate	aggressive	progression	centigrade	gradual

to move a **step** in a positive direction; to improve; to move a **step** closer to a goal	to move up a **step** or level; to improve in quality
to stray away from the main topic; to **step** away from the topic and lose clarity; to wander in thoughts or ideas	a slow change; a **step-by-step** change
to move up a **step** in education (usually out of a school)	to reduce someone's worth or value; to make someone **step** down to a lower position or rank; to move down a **step** in social status
Celsius; temperature rating on the thermometer made up of 100 degree intervals or **steps** between the freezing and boiling points of water	to go back; to move backward; to move a **step** back
a **step-by-step** sequence within a continuous series	hostile; pushy; **stepping** into someone's space with forceful energy

More Greek and Latin Roots • 4–8 © 2007 Creative Teaching Press

Read-Around Review: grad, gress

I have the first card. Who has the roots that mean **step**?	I have the word **progress**. Who has the word that names what people do when they finish all the **steps** or grades in high school?
I have the roots **grad** and **gress**. Who has the word that describes what a person does when they wander off the subject in the middle of a conversation?	I have the word **graduate**. Who has the word that describes a **step** backward?
I have the word **digress**. Who has the word that describes what happens when a person gets to change from coach to a first-class seat on an airplane?	I have the word **regress**. Who has the word that means to reduce someone's value or status, such as when a person puts down another person?
I have the word **upgrade**. Who has the word that describes a slow **step-by-step** change, such as the melting of an ice cube?	I have the word **degrade**. Who has the word that describes a **step-by-step** sequence?
I have the word **gradual**. Who has the word that names the degree intervals on a thermometer from 0–100?	I have the word **progression**. Who has the word that describes a person who shows force or hostility toward someone else?
I have the word **centigrade**. Who has the word that means to move a **step** in a positive direction or when a person is making improvements in something?	I have the word **aggressive**. Who has the first card?

Name _____   Date _____

Vocabulary Quiz: grad, gress

Shade in the bubble for the correct word.

1 The two neighbors showed *this* towards one another when they began arguing in the driveway.
   Ⓐ **aggression**   Ⓑ **digression**   Ⓒ **regression**   Ⓓ **progression**

2 The temperature reached 80 degrees Celsius on Sunday. "Which word below names the temperature degree intervals?"
   Ⓐ **digression**   Ⓑ **progression**   Ⓒ **regression**   Ⓓ **centigrade**

3 Mrs. Jones attended the ceremony that celebrated her daughter finishing high school. "What did she attend?"
   Ⓐ **aggression**   Ⓑ **graduation**   Ⓒ **regression**   Ⓓ **degrading**

4 The puppy slowly fell asleep in his new owner's arms. "What word below describes how the puppy fell asleep?"
   Ⓐ **gradually**   Ⓑ **upgrading**   Ⓒ **aggressive**   Ⓓ **regression**

5 Although he was 90 years old, the man's disease caused him to do *this* and act like a child.
   Ⓐ **progress**   Ⓑ **regress**   Ⓒ **graduate**   Ⓓ **upgrade**

6 Joe felt *this* after receiving an insulting comment that made him feel like he was being treated like a child.
   Ⓐ **upgraded**   Ⓑ **gradual**   Ⓒ **degraded**   Ⓓ **regression**

7 Sarah's hotel room was *this* when it was changed from a small room to a large suite.
   Ⓐ **degraded**   Ⓑ **digressed**   Ⓒ **gradual**   Ⓓ **upgraded**

8 Katie was getting closer to meeting her goals. "What word below describes her positive movement?"
   Ⓐ **progressing**   Ⓑ **digressing**   Ⓒ **degrading**   Ⓓ **graduating**

9 What word below describes what happens when a detailed and informative story starts to wander off topic?
   Ⓐ **digresses**   Ⓑ **degrades**   Ⓒ **progresses**   Ⓓ **regresses**

10 The grocery store clerk demonstrated *this* by making step-by-step movements toward becoming a store manager.
   Ⓐ **aggression**   Ⓑ **degrading**   Ⓒ **progression**   Ⓓ **digression**

Write the correct word on the line so that the sentence makes sense and sounds grammatically correct.

11 The student was sent to the principal's office for being too _____ with another student at lunch.

12 It feels _____ when someone puts you down.

13 The temperature was _____ increasing a few degrees _____ every hour.

14 It is more important to make _____ than it is to simply do well.

15 We are _____ our tickets for the concert from the back row to the second row!

More Greek and Latin Roots • 4–8 © 2007 Creative Teaching Press

Name _____   Date _____

Review Test: mob, mot, mov, grad, gress

Write the correct word from the word bank to complete each sentence.

1 The purpose of television commercials is to _____ the benefits of a product so more people will buy it.

2 After Danielle's third year of violin lessons, her parents could hear the _____ she was making as she played a difficult song by Mozart.

3 The manager had to _____ his employee when he found out that the man had made many mistakes.

4 Would you like me to _____ your rental car from a small compact car to a large SUV?

5 At her eighth grade _____ party, Maria sang her favorite song, "Off to High School," on the karaoke machine.

6 Giving someone an incentive might help _____ him or her to do something that is challenging.

7 The Kominskys rented a dump truck to speed up the _____ of all the dirt in preparation for the construction of their new pool.

8 One day the rock star had white hair, but it was black the very next day! That hair color change sure wasn't _____!

9 It's important to practice self-control at all times so that there won't be any problems with _____ toward others.

10 As a result of her fractured wrist, Mandy would have no _____ of her arm for six weeks while it was healing in the cast.

11 It was hard to understand the speaker's message at the conference, because he kept _____ to other topics.

12 When his baby brother was born, Kyle _____ and used "baby talk" to seek attention from his parents.

13 If you ever think about saying something unkind about someone else, just remember how _____ it makes you feel.

14 We need to _____ the members of our Girl Scout troop so that we can prepare for this year's sale of cookies.

15 It was so fun watching the _____ of the parade as it marched down Main Street.

Word Bank
aggression
automobile
centigrade
degraded
demote
digressing
gradual
graduation
locomotion
mobile
mobility
mobilize
motion
motivate
progress
progression
promote
regressed
removal
upgrade

Word List: pos = to place, put

Vocabulary	Definitions
apposition (n)	a word or phrase **placed** next to another word in order to define or identify it
compose (v)	to **put** ideas into writing; to write a musical piece; to create or produce
depose (v)	to remove from office or power; to take out of **place**; to **put** down
deposit (v)	to **put** money into an account
expose (v)	to **put** something out for others to see
imposition (n)	something that is a burden to someone else; to **put** your needs above someone else's to the point that it's a burden for others
juxtapose (v)	**to place** side-by-side for the purpose of comparing and contrasting
post (v)	to **put** something up on a board for everyone to see; to display
proposal (n)	a plan or offer that is usually **put** down in writing
transpose (v)	to **put** into a different order or place; to reverse or transfer the order

More Greek and Latin Roots • 4–8 © 2007 Creative Teaching Press

Vocabulary Sort: pos

imposition	proposal	expose	deposit	juxtapose
depose	post	transpose	compose	apposition

something that is a burden to someone else; to **put** your needs above someone else's to the point that it's a burden for others	**to place** side-by-side for the purpose of comparing and contrasting
a word or phrase **placed** next to another word in order to define or identify it	a plan or offer that is usually **put** down in writing
to **put** ideas into writing; to write a musical piece; to create or produce	to **put** something out for others to see
to remove from office or power; to take out of **place**; to **put** down	to **put** money into an account
to **put** something up on a board for everyone to see; to display	to **put** into a different order or place; to reverse or transfer the order

Read-Around Review: pos

I have the first card.

Who has the root that means
to place or **put**?

I have the word **expose**.

Who has the word that describes what
a person creates when they ask someone
else for a favor on short notice?

I have the root **pos**.

Who has the word that means to **put**
things into a different order, such as mixing
letters around in a word when writing?

I have the word **imposition**.

Who has the word that describes
putting money into an account, often
with the purpose of saving it?

I have the word **transpose**.

Who has the word that means to create
something that often requires creativity,
such as a story?

I have the word **deposit**.

Who has the word that names
the noun or phrase that identifies or
defines the noun it follows?

I have the word **compose**.

Who has the word that means to **put**
things next to each other in order to
analyze similarities and differences?

I have the word **apposition**.

Who has the word that describes
what people do when they remove
someone from power?

I have the word **juxtapose**.

Who has the word that names
what you are doing when you hang
a notice on a bulletin board?

I have the word **depose**.

Who has the word that identifies a plan
or offer that is usually written down?

I have the word **post**.

Who has the word that means
to **put** something out for others
to see in careful detail?

I have the word **proposal**.

Who has the first card?

More Greek and Latin Roots • 4–8 © 2007 Creative Teaching Press

Vocabulary Quiz: pos

Shade in the bubble for the correct word.

1. Many people use journals to write down their thoughts and ideas to do *this*.
   - Ⓐ **deposit**
   - Ⓑ **post**
   - Ⓒ **compose**
   - Ⓓ **depose**

2. Tracie's mom agreed to her daughter's idea or *this* to have a sleepover to celebrate Tracie's birthday.
   - Ⓐ **apposition**
   - Ⓑ **proposal**
   - Ⓒ **transpose**
   - Ⓓ **imposition**

3. Ben often did *this* with his numbers and reversed the order when writing them down.
   - Ⓐ **transposed**
   - Ⓑ **deposed**
   - Ⓒ **composed**
   - Ⓓ **juxtaposed**

4. John said, "Wow! We need to hang this letter on the wall for everyone to see!" "What will he do with the letter?"
   - Ⓐ **juxtapose**
   - Ⓑ **compose**
   - Ⓒ **impose**
   - Ⓓ **post**

5. Ashleigh did *this* with her money when she put it in her bank account.
   - Ⓐ **deposited**
   - Ⓑ **exposed**
   - Ⓒ **posted**
   - Ⓓ **transposed**

6. What word below describes a situation that inconveniences someone?
   - Ⓐ **imposition**
   - Ⓑ **exposed**
   - Ⓒ **juxtaposed**
   - Ⓓ **apposition**

7. People with fair complexions can burn after a few minutes of being in the sun. "In what state is their skin when this happens?"
   - Ⓐ **juxtapose**
   - Ⓑ **exposed**
   - Ⓒ **apposition**
   - Ⓓ **composed**

8. The people did *this* to the leader when they removed him from office because he treated his people poorly.
   - Ⓐ **imposition**
   - Ⓑ **transposed**
   - Ⓒ **deposited**
   - Ⓓ **deposed**

9. Dave's dog, Shiloh, loves to go for walks in the park. "What is the word *Shiloh* in this sentence?"
   - Ⓐ **an apposition**
   - Ⓑ **a posting**
   - Ⓒ **a deposit**
   - Ⓓ **a proposal**

10. The interior decorator placed the two paintings next to each other to decide which one to use. "What word below describes what she did?"
    - Ⓐ **juxtaposed**
    - Ⓑ **imposed**
    - Ⓒ **transposed**
    - Ⓓ **posted**

Write the correct word on the line so that the sentence makes sense and sounds grammatically correct.

11. I'm sorry for the _____, but could I stay at your house for a week while I get new carpet installed?

12. The chef did not want the ingredients of his secret recipe _____.

13. Many businesses will _____ their job openings in newspapers and on the Internet.

14. Dawn wrote down her ideas for a book, and then submitted the _____ to the publishing company.

15. Eric wanted to _____ a letter to his friend, but he didn't know what to say.

Word List: sed, sid, sess = to sit, settle

Vocabulary	Definitions
assessor (n)	an official who evaluates and **settles** on a value of a property for tax purposes
president (n)	an executive officer who **sits** in charge of a firm or organization
reside (v)	to **settle** into a place to live; to exist
residence (n)	a home; a place where a person **settles** to live
sedan (n)	a closed automobile that has enough room for four people **to sit** comfortably
sedate (v)	to help someone calm down; to help someone **settle** down
sedative (n)	medicine used to help a person **settle** into a state of calmness
sedentary (adj)	fixed to one spot; marked by a great deal of **sitting** and very little exercise or travel
sediment (n)	the solid material that **settles** to the bottom of a liquid
session (n)	a meeting, class, or assembly where a group **sits** together

THE PRESIDENT

More Greek and Latin Roots • 4–8 © 2007 Creative Teaching Press

Vocabulary Sort: sed, sid, sess

sedentary	reside	sedate	sediment	session
assessor	president	sedan	residence	sedative

to **settle** into a place to live; to exist	an official who evaluates and **settles** on a value of a property for tax purposes
the solid material that **settles** to the bottom of a liquid	to help someone calm down; to help someone **settle** down
a closed automobile that has enough room for four people **to sit** comfortably	an executive officer who **sits** in charge of a firm or organization
a home; a place where a person **settles** to live	fixed to one spot; marked by a great deal of **sitting** and very little exercise or travel
medicine used to help a person **settle** into a state of calmness	a meeting, class, or assembly where a group **sits** together

Read-Around Review: sed, sid, sess

I have the first card.

Who has the roots that mean **to sit** or **settle**?

I have the word **sedentary**.

Who has the word that identifies an executive officer in charge of a firm or organization?

I have the roots **sed, sid, sess**.

Who has the word that means a meeting or class where people **sit** together?

I have the word **president**.

Who has the word that identifies the solid material that **settles** to the bottom of a liquid?

I have the word **session**.

Who has the word that identifies the medicine used to calm a person down?

I have the word **sediment**.

Who has the word that names an official who **settles** on values of property for tax purposes?

I have the word **sedative**.

Who has the word that names a home or a place where a person lives?

I have the word **assessor**.

Who has the word that describes what you do when you **settle** into a place to live?

I have the word **residence**.

Who has the word that names a closed automobile with enough room for at least four people to ride comfortably?

I have the word **reside**.

Who has the word that identifies what you are doing when you try to calm someone down?

I have the word **sedan**.

Who has the word that describes a lifestyle in which a person spends most of the time **sitting** around being inactive?

I have the word **sedate**.

Who has the first card?

More Greek and Latin Roots • 4–8 © 2007 Creative Teaching Press

Name _____   Date _____

Vocabulary Quiz: sed, sid, sess

Shade in the bubble for the correct word.

1 After the car accident, the doctor gave *this* to the driver to calm him down.
 Ⓐ **sedentary**   Ⓑ **sedative**   Ⓒ **session**   Ⓓ **residence**

2 People have this kind of lifestyle if they are inactive and never exercise.
 Ⓐ **sedentary**   Ⓑ **sedate**   Ⓒ **sedan**   Ⓓ **president**

3 After leaving her fruit smoothie sitting on the counter, Jasmine noticed that the bits of fruit had settled to the bottom. "What do you call the pieces that settled to the bottom?"
 Ⓐ **reside**   Ⓑ **sedate**   Ⓒ **sedan**   Ⓓ **sediment**

4 Mary's car has enough room for four people to ride to the movie together. "What type of car does she have?"
 Ⓐ **sedan**   Ⓑ **residence**   Ⓒ **session**   Ⓓ **assessor**

5 At the end of the meeting, the speaker asked if there were any questions. "What is another word for *meeting*?"
 Ⓐ **sedate**   Ⓑ **sediment**   Ⓒ **sedative**   Ⓓ **session**

6 Lucy's veterinarian recommended she do *this* to her dog to keep him calm during the plane ride.
 Ⓐ **sedate**   Ⓑ **sediment**   Ⓒ **reside**   Ⓓ **sedentary**

7 What is another name for your home or place where you live?
 Ⓐ **sedative**   Ⓑ **reside**   Ⓒ **sedan**   Ⓓ **residence**

8 The county is sending someone out to determine how much our home is worth. "What do you call this person?"
 Ⓐ **sedentary**   Ⓑ **assessor**   Ⓒ **sedate**   Ⓓ **sedative**

9 Heather was promoted and will be in charge of the company. "What will be the name of her title?"
 Ⓐ **sedentary**   Ⓑ **session**   Ⓒ **president**   Ⓓ **sedan**

10 Some college students live on campus. "What is another word for *live*?"
 Ⓐ **reside**   Ⓑ **session**   Ⓒ **sediment**   Ⓓ **sedentary**

Write the correct word on the line so that the sentence makes sense and sounds grammatically correct.

11 We are moving to a _____ that was just built in the new community.

12 Only people who registered for the meeting will be allowed to enter the closed _____ to hear the guest speakers.

13 The doctor gave his patient a _____ to help calm his nerves.

14 There was some _____ at the bottom of his bottle of juice.

15 The opposite of an active lifestyle is a _____ lifestyle.

More Greek and Latin Roots • 4–8 © 2007 Creative Teaching Press

Name _____   Date _____

Review Test: pos, sed, sid, sess

Write the correct word from the word bank to complete each sentence.

1 I'm on my way to _____ my birthday money into my college savings account.

2 Henry decided to trade in his compact car for a _____ large enough to fit his dog safely and comfortably in the back seat.

3 The new _____ of Congress will begin in two weeks.

4 Many readers were surprised to find that the magician was willing to _____ the secrets to his magic tricks.

5 If she knew what an _____ it was, she would not have asked for a ride to school.

6 Jessie did not want to drink the juice because there was _____ at the bottom of the glass.

7 Did you remember to include your e-mail address on the memo before you _____ it on the corkboard?

8 Only a doctor or nurse should _____ another person with medication.

9 The musician was in the middle of _____ her first song.

10 The residents of the small town drafted a _____ for a dog park to be built in the town square.

11 As they age, even the most active animals develop more _____ lifestyles.

12 The art critic wanted to _____ the two paintings so that he could more clearly identify how the elements differed.

13 Next year, I get to _____ in Paris while attending college abroad for the semester.

14 I thought the phone number had been disconnected, but I simply _____ the digits and called the wrong number.

15 My new _____ is only two blocks from school, so now I'll get to walk with my friends.

apposition
assessor
composing
depose
deposit
expose
imposition
juxtapose
posted
president
proposal
reside
residence
sedan
sedate
sedative
sedentary
sediment
session
transposed

More Greek and Latin Roots • 4–8 © 2007 Creative Teaching Press

Word List: log = word, idea, reason, speech

Vocabulary	Definitions
analogy (n)	**words** that draw comparisons and similarities
apology (n)	**words** expressing regret; **words** asking to be excused for an action
dialog (n)	a conversation between two or more people; **words** shared between people
epilogue (n)	a short section added to the end of a book; a short poem or **speech** directly to the audience at the end of a play
eulogy (n)	kind **words** spoken about a person who has passed away; high praise
logbook (n)	an official record; a book in which information is written in a timely manner
logical (adj)	a statement, thought, or action that is **reasonable**; **words** that make sense
logo (n)	a **word**, name, symbol, or trademark designed for easy recognition
monologue (n)	a long **speech** made by one person; a continuous series of jokes delivered by a comedian
prologue (n)	introduction; preface; an introductory chapter at the beginning of a book or play

More Greek and Latin Roots • 4–8 © 2007 Creative Teaching Press

Vocabulary Sort: log

monologue	eulogy	logo	dialog	prologue
logical	apology	logbook	analogy	epilogue

a **word**, name, symbol, or trademark designed for easy recognition	a conversation between two or more people; **words** shared between people
introduction; preface; an introductory chapter at the beginning of a book or play	a short section added to the end of a book; a short poem or **speech** directly to the audience at the end of a play
words expressing regret; **words** asking to be excused for an action	**words** that draw comparisons and similarities
an official record; a book in which information is written in a timely manner	kind **words** spoken about a person who has passed away; high praise
a long **speech** made by one person; a continuous series of jokes delivered by a comedian	a statement, thought, or action that is **reasonable**; **words** that make sense

More Greek and Latin Roots • 4–8 © 2007 Creative Teaching Press

Read-Around Review: log

I have the first card.

Who has the root that means **word**, **idea**, **reason**, or **speech**?

I have the word **eulogy**.

Who has the word that describes an item that contains records, such as a ship's destination and course?

I have the root **log**.

Who has the word that identifies a **word**, image, icon, or trademark that corresponds to a company or brand for easy recognition?

I have the word **logbook**.

Who has the word that names the introductory chapter of a book?

I have the word **logo**.

Who has the word that means the same thing as a conversation between two or more people?

I have the word **prologue**.

Who has the word that compares **words** or **ideas** to see how they are similar?

I have the word **dialog**.

Who has the word that names a long **speech** made by one person?

I have the word **analogy**.

Who has the word that identifies what you are offering if you say, "I'm sorry"?

I have the word **monologue**.

Who has the word that describes something that is **reasonable** and makes sense?

I have the word **apology**.

Who has the word that identifies a short section added to the end of a book that usually tells what happened later?

I have the word **logical**.

Who has the word that identifies a **speech** of kind remembrance for a person who has passed away?

I have the word **epilogue**.

Who has the first card?

More Greek and Latin Roots • 4–8 © 2007 Creative Teaching Press

Name _____   Date _____

Vocabulary Quiz: log

Shade in the bubble for the correct word.

1 A friend gives *this* when he or she offers words of regret after hurting another person's feelings unintentionally.
Ⓐ **apology**   Ⓑ **eulogy**   Ⓒ **analogy**   Ⓓ **logo**

2 This extra section in the book explained what happened to the main character 20 years later.
Ⓐ **monologue**   Ⓑ **prologue**   Ⓒ **dialog**   Ⓓ **epilogue**

3 The pharmacist records all of the prescriptions distributed each day in *this*.
Ⓐ **logbook**   Ⓑ **prologue**   Ⓒ **analogy**   Ⓓ **dialog**

4 Many late-night talk shows begin with the host delivering a long comedic speech. "What is this called?"
Ⓐ **epilogue**   Ⓑ **prologue**   Ⓒ **eulogy**   Ⓓ **monologue**

5 Jeff gave a memorable speech at his grandmother's funeral. "What is this speech called?"
Ⓐ **eulogy**   Ⓑ **monologue**   Ⓒ **dialog**   Ⓓ **epilogue**

6 The company had this familiar image stamped onto all products to reinforce it in the minds of the customers.
Ⓐ **logo**   Ⓑ **prologue**   Ⓒ **analogy**   Ⓓ **epilogue**

7 Linda's conclusion was reasonable based on the data. "What word below describes Linda's conclusion?"
Ⓐ **monologue**   Ⓑ **dialog**   Ⓒ **analogy**   Ⓓ **logical**

8 The telephone is a common mode for having a conversation or *this* with a friend.
Ⓐ **dialog**   Ⓑ **epilogue**   Ⓒ **monologue**   Ⓓ **eulogy**

9 Some books include this introductory chapter telling the reader about the lives of the characters before the book begins.
Ⓐ **epilogue**   Ⓑ **eulogy**   Ⓒ **dialog**   Ⓓ **prologue**

10 *Dangerous* is to *safe* as *open* is to *closed* is an example of what?
Ⓐ **analogy**   Ⓑ **logo**   Ⓒ **dialog**   Ⓓ **eulogy**

Write the correct word on the line so that the sentence makes sense and sounds grammatically correct.

11 The teacher had a _____ with Amanda about her poor test grade.

12 Liz's design for the new company _____ would be featured on all of their materials.

13 My teacher made an _____ between school and the workplace stating that honesty, hard work, and perseverance were important in both situations.

14 The novel included a _____ describing the previous mysteries the detective had solved.

15 The priest delivered a heartfelt _____ on behalf of his friend who had passed away unexpectedly.

More Greek and Latin Roots • 4–8 © 2007 Creative Teaching Press

Word List: ono, nym, onym = word, name

Vocabulary	Definitions
acronym (n)	an abbreviation formed by combining the initial letters in **words** or parts of a series of **words**
anonymous (adj)	not **named** or identified; done by someone unknown
antonym (n)	a **word** that means the opposite of another **word**
eponym (n)	a person for whom something, such as a city, building, or street, has been **named**
heteronym (n)	one of two or more **words** that are spelled alike but have different meanings and pronunciations, such as *bass voice* and *bass, a fish*
homonym (n)	one of two or more **words** that are pronounced alike but have different spellings and meanings, such as *isle* and *aisle*
onomatopoeia (n)	the formation of **words** that imitate sounds associated with the objects or actions to which they refer
oronym (n)	a string of **words** that sounds the same as another string of **words**, such as *gray day* and *grade A*
pseudonym (n)	false **name**; a fictitious **name**
synonym (n)	one of two or more **words** that have the same meaning

More Greek and Latin Roots • 4–8 © 2007 Creative Teaching Press

Vocabulary Sort: ono, nym, onym

pseudonym	homonym	eponym	oronym	acronym
anonymous	synonym	heteronym	antonym	onomatopoeia

a person for whom something, such as a city, building, or street has been **named**	a string of **words** that sounds the same as another string of **words**, such as *gray day* and *grade A*
an abbreviation formed by combining the initial letters of **words** or parts of a series of **words**	a **word** that means the opposite of another **word**
the formation of **words** that imitate sounds associated with the objects or actions to which they refer	not **named** or identified; done by someone unknown
false **name**; a fictitious **name**	one of two or more **words** that have the same meaning
one of two or more **words** that are pronounced alike but have different spellings and meanings, such as *isle* and *aisle*	one of two or more **words** that are spelled alike but have different meanings and pronunciations, such as *bass voice* and *bass, a fish*

More Greek and Latin Roots • 4–8 © 2007 Creative Teaching Press

Read-Around Review: ono, nym, onym

I have the first card. Who has the roots that mean **word** or **name**?	I have the word **onomatopoeia**. Who has the word that describes an unknown person that has done something, such as write a book?
I have the roots **ono**, **nym** and **onym**. Who has the word that names two strings of **words** that sound similar, such as "I scream" and "ice cream"?	I have the word **anonymous**. Who has the word for a person after whom something was **named**, such as Amerigo Vespucci, from whom we get *America*?
I have the word **oronym**. Who has the word that names **words** with identical spellings but different meanings and pronunciations?	I have the word **eponym**. Who has the word that means a fictitious **name** used by authors who want to hide their identities?
I have the word **heteronym**. Who has the word that names a **word** that has the opposite meaning of another word?	I have the word **pseudonym**. Who has the word that means a **word** that has the same meaning as another word?
I have the word **antonym**. Who has the word that names **words** that sound the same but have different meanings and spellings?	I have the word **synonym**. Who has the word that describes the letters *PTA* meaning *Parent Teacher Association*?
I have the word **homonym**. Who has the word that names a **word** that imitates the sound of an object, such as "buzz" for a bee?	I have the word **acronym**. Who has the first card?

More Greek and Latin Roots • 4–8 © 2007 Creative Teaching Press

Vocabulary Quiz: ono, nym, onym

Shade in the bubble for the correct word.

1. Some authors prefer not to be identified. They would prefer to remain *this*.
   - Ⓐ **eponym**
   - Ⓑ **acronym**
   - Ⓒ **oronym**
   - Ⓓ **anonymous**

2. Theodor Geisel enjoyed using *these*, or various names, such as Theo LeSieg and Dr. Seuss.
   - Ⓐ **synonyms**
   - Ⓑ **eponyms**
   - Ⓒ **homonyms**
   - Ⓓ **pseudonyms**

3. Which word below identifies a word that imitates the sound it represents, such as *clang*, *meow*, or *moo*?
   - Ⓐ **heteronym**
   - Ⓑ **onomatopoeia**
   - Ⓒ **antonym**
   - Ⓓ **eponym**

4. "That factory will *produce* most of the *produce* needed by the entire country?" "*Produce* is an example of what type of word?"
   - Ⓐ **heteronym**
   - Ⓑ **homonym**
   - Ⓒ **eponym**
   - Ⓓ **acronym**

5. "The stuffy nose can be a bother," and "the stuff he knows can be a bother" are examples of what type of words?
   - Ⓐ **oronyms**
   - Ⓑ **acronyms**
   - Ⓒ **homonyms**
   - Ⓓ **eponyms**

6. The words *excellent* and *outstanding* have similar meanings? "What do we call these types of words?"
   - Ⓐ **synonyms**
   - Ⓑ **antonyms**
   - Ⓒ **homonyms**
   - Ⓓ **acronyms**

7. The NBA stands for the National Basketball Association. "NBA is an example of what type of word?"
   - Ⓐ **eponym**
   - Ⓑ **homonym**
   - Ⓒ **onomatopoeia**
   - Ⓓ **acronym**

8. The words *generous* and *selfish* have opposite meanings. "What do we call these types of words?"
   - Ⓐ **heteronyms**
   - Ⓑ **eponyms**
   - Ⓒ **anonymous**
   - Ⓓ **antonyms**

9. What type of words are illustrated in the following sentence? "I need a *weather* update so I know *whether* or not to pack shorts."
   - Ⓐ **homonyms**
   - Ⓑ **eponyms**
   - Ⓒ **onomatopoeia**
   - Ⓓ **antonyms**

10. Alzheimer's disease was named after Dr. Alois Alzheimer (1864–1915), because he was the first to identify the symptoms of the disease. "This is an example of what word?"
    - Ⓐ **oronym**
    - Ⓑ **eponym**
    - Ⓒ **antonym**
    - Ⓓ **acronym**

Write the correct name for each set of examples.

11. *Hot* and *cold*, and *unkind* and *friendly* are examples of _____.

12. *Teas* and *tease*, and *wail* and *whale* are examples of _____.

13. *CSI*, *NASA*, *CIA*, and *FBI* are examples of _____.

14. I had to take (a nice; an ice) cold shower is an example of an _____.

15. *Delicious* and *tasty*, and *speedy* and *fast* are examples of _____.

More Greek and Latin Roots • 4–8 © 2007 Creative Teaching Press

Review Test: log, ono, nym, onym

Write the correct word from the word bank to complete each sentence.

1. The captain of the cruise ship required his workers to keep a _____ of the ports they visited.

2. Some common _____ include MPH, RBI, and RSVP.

3. The author of the recipes chose to remain _____ rather than have his privacy jeopardized by e-mails and visitors to his home.

4. At the funeral, there was a touching _____ presented by the members of the orchestra in which he played for 20 years.

5. I could hear the birds chirping outside my window. "What type of word is *chirping*?" _____

6. The cereal company hired an advertising agency to create an updated _____ in the hopes that the consumers would soon associate the image with the delicious products.

7. The words *save* and *spend* are examples of what kind of words? _____

8. Your story is exciting, but you need to find a _____ for the word "cool." It's not proper to use slang in a piece of writing.

9. The beverage called the Shirley Temple is an _____ because it was named after the famous actress.

10. I will accept your _____ only if you promise never to do it to me again.

11. The famous child actress from *The Wizard of Oz* was really named Frances Ethel Gumm. She chose to use *Judy Garland* as her _____ in the acting world.

12. A _____ solution to a problem is one that makes sense.

13. The author explained what happened after the story ended in the _____ after the last chapter.

14. She *led* the fight to remove *lead* from the manufacturing process in creating pencils. "What are *led* and *lead*?" _____

15. Before beginning the first chapter, Kimberly read the _____ to determine what happened to the same characters in the other books of the series.

Word Bank:

acronyms
analogy
anonymous
antonyms
apology
dialog
epilogue
eponym
eulogy
heteronym
homonyms
logbook
logical
logo
monologue
onomatopoeia
oronym
prologue
pseudonym
synonym

Word List: tain, ten, tent = hold

Vocabulary	Definitions
abstain (v)	to **hold** back from an activity by choice; to **hold** back from voting
contain (v)	to **hold**; to have within
detain (v)	to **hold** back; to delay; to keep from proceeding
detention (n)	a period of time in which someone is **held** back; a form of punishment by **holding** someone after school hours
extend (v)	to **hold** out; to unbend; to stretch or spread out; to offer
patent (n)	legal ownership of an invention **held** by the creator; exclusive right or ownership
retainer (n)	something that **holds** something else in; a device that **holds** something in
tenant (n)	a **holder** of land rights; a person who **holds** the right to live in a residence; an occupant
tendon (n)	a band of tough fibrous tissue that **holds** a muscle to a bone
tentative (adj)	**holding** back on the final decision; uncertain; hesitant; not fully agreed upon

More Greek and Latin Roots • 4–8 © 2007 Creative Teaching Press

Vocabulary Sort: tain, ten, tent

contain	patent	abstain	extend	tentative
tendon	retainer	tenant	detention	detain

to **hold** back; to delay; to keep from proceeding	a period of time in which someone is **held** back; a form of punishment by **holding** someone after school hours
to **hold** out; to unbend; to stretch or spread out; to offer	legal ownership of an invention **held** by the creator; exclusive right or ownership
a **holder** of land rights; a person who **holds** the right to live in a residence; an occupant	to **hold** back from an activity by choice; to **hold** back from voting
to **hold**; to have within	a band of tough fibrous tissue that **holds** a muscle to a bone
holding back on the final decision; uncertain; hesitant; not fully agreed upon	something that **holds** something else in; a device that **holds** something in

Read-Around Review: tain, ten, tent

I have the first card.

Who has the roots that mean to **hold**?

I have the word **tendon**.

Who has the word that identifies a device, that has the purpose of **holding** something in place?

I have the roots **tain**, **ten**, **tent**.

Who has the word that identifies what you **hold** if you invented something and have legal ownership of it?

I have the word **retainer**.

Who has the word that means to **hold** something in?

I have the word **patent**.

Who has the word that identifies a person who **holds** the right to live in a home or on a specific piece of land?

I have the word **contain**.

Who has the word that means uncertain or undecided?

I have the word **tenant**.

Who has the word that means to stretch out?

I have the word **tentative**.

Who has the word that means to **hold** back on doing something by choice?

I have the word **extend**.

Who has the word that names the punishment you receive when you have to stay after school?

I have the word **abstain**.

Who has the word that means to delay or to **hold** someone back?

I have the word **detention**.

Who has the word that names the body part made up of tissue that connects muscles to bones?

I have the word **detain**.

Who has the first card?

More Greek and Latin Roots • 4–8 © 2007 Creative Teaching Press

Name _____   Date _____

Vocabulary Quiz: tain, ten, tent

Shade in the bubble for the correct word.

1 Tori reached out to shake the hand of her new classmate. "What did she do with her arm?"
    Ⓐ **retainer**   Ⓑ **tentative**   Ⓒ **extend**   Ⓓ **patent**

2 Lucy had to hold back on voting because her mom was one of the candidates. "What did Lucy do?"
    Ⓐ **abstain**   Ⓑ **tenant**   Ⓒ **detain**   Ⓓ **contain**

3 John tore a piece of *this* tissue, so his arm was placed in a cast for six weeks while it mended.
    Ⓐ **tenant**   Ⓑ **tendon**   Ⓒ **detention**   Ⓓ **retainer**

4 The owner of the property was looking for a person to rent his home. "Who was the owner looking for?"
    Ⓐ **retainer**   Ⓑ **contain**   Ⓒ **tenant**   Ⓓ **patent**

5 The passenger was delayed from boarding the plane for safety reasons. "What did the airline officials do with the passenger?"
    Ⓐ **detained**   Ⓑ **contained**   Ⓒ **tentative**   Ⓓ **abstained**

6 The inventor of the motorized robotic floor mop filed for *this* so she would have sole ownership.
    Ⓐ **retainer**   Ⓑ **container**   Ⓒ **patent**   Ⓓ **tenant**

7 After having her braces removed, Abigail was instructed to wear this device every night to hold her teeth in place.
    Ⓐ **patent**   Ⓑ **tendon**   Ⓒ **container**   Ⓓ **retainer**

8 What word below describes Tim and Troy's unconfirmed plans to have dinner at the new restaurant?
    Ⓐ **tentative**   Ⓑ **detention**   Ⓒ **patent**   Ⓓ **detained**

9 When Cari forgot her homework two days in a row, she was given this punishment of staying after school.
    Ⓐ **abstain**   Ⓑ **tendon**   Ⓒ **tentative**   Ⓓ **detention**

10 The movie was so funny that it was hard for Jake to keep his laughter to himself. "What could Jake not do with his laughter?"
    Ⓐ **contain**   Ⓑ **detain**   Ⓒ **retain**   Ⓓ **abstain**

Write the correct word on the line so that the sentence makes sense and sounds grammatically correct.

11 I'd like to _____ an invitation for you and your family to join me at the party.

12 Mandy couldn't wait to open her present. She wondered what the tiny blue box might _____.

13 In order to stay healthy, many adults _____ from drinking anything other than juice, milk, tea, or water.

14 Due to the unexpected ice storm, the plane was _____ at the airport for three hours.

15 Would you like to make _____ plans to join me at the skate park this weekend?

Word List: fer = to carry, bear, bring together

Vocabulary	Definitions
chauffeur (n)	a person hired to drive or **bring** someone to another location; a driver
circumference (n)	the distance around a circle; **to carry** the distance around a circle
conference (n)	a meeting that **brings** people **together** to exchange views or information
differ (v)	**to carry** a different opinion; **to carry** an opposing view
fertile (adj)	capable of **bearing** or producing crops or vegetation; highly productive
infer (v)	to **bring together** information to reach a conclusion; guess
offer (v)	to **bring** forth ideas; to propose or present
prefer (v)	to choose one thing that **carries** priority over another; to value more highly
referral (n)	a recommendation; a letter or notice that **carries** good words about a person
transfer (v)	to **bring** something from one place to another

More Greek and Latin Roots • 4–8 © 2007 Creative Teaching Press

Vocabulary Sort: fer

referral	transfer	differ	fertile	conference
circumference	chauffeur	prefer	offer	infer

to carry a different opinion; **to carry** an opposing view	a meeting that **brings** people **together** to exchange views or information
to **bring together** information to reach a conclusion; guess	to choose one thing that **carries** priority over another; to value more highly
a person hired to drive or **bring** someone to another location; a driver	the distance around a circle; **to carry** the distance around a circle
a recommendation; a letter or notice that **carries** good words about a person	to **bring** forth ideas; to propose or present
to **bring** something from one place to another	capable of **bearing** or producing crops or vegetation; highly productive

More Greek and Latin Roots • 4–8 © 2007 Creative Teaching Press

Read-Around Review: fer

I have the first card. Who has the root that means **to carry**, **bear**, or **bring together**?	I have the word **transfer**. Who has the word that means to put information **together** to draw a conclusion, as you often do when reading great books?
I have the root **fer**. Who has the word that identifies a recommendation for a job?	I have the word **infer**. Who has the word that means to disagree with someone's ideas?
I have the word **referral**. Who has the word that identifies or describes what you do when you propose an idea or suggestion?	I have the word **differ**. Who has the word that identifies the distance around a circle?
I have the word **offer**. Who has the word that means that you would rather do one thing than another?	I have the word **circumference**. Who has the word that describes land that will **bear** fruit, crops, or other vegetation due to its rich soil?
I have the word **prefer**. Who has the word that identifies a meeting in which people have usually come to learn something?	I have the word **fertile**. Who has the word that identifies a person who will **bring** you from one place to another, often in a limousine?
I have the word **conference**. Who has the word that means to move or **carry** something from one place to another?	I have the word **chauffeur**. Who has the first card?

More Greek and Latin Roots • 4–8 © 2007 Creative Teaching Press

Name _____   Date _____

Vocabulary Quiz: fer

Shade in the bubble for the correct word.

1 Rick scheduled this person to pick him up at the airport and drive him to his hotel.
    Ⓐ **chauffeur**   Ⓑ **transfer**   Ⓒ **differ**   Ⓓ **prefer**

2 People's opinions often do *this* when discussing politics.
    Ⓐ **referral**   Ⓑ **transfer**   Ⓒ **infer**   Ⓓ **differ**

3 Amy suggested decorating the room with balloons for the party. "What did she do with her idea?"
    Ⓐ **differed**   Ⓑ **infered**   Ⓒ **offered**   Ⓓ **transfered**

4 The dentist gave Dave *this* when he recommended the name of an orthodontist for Dave's crooked teeth.
    Ⓐ **referral**   Ⓑ **transfer**   Ⓒ **differ**   Ⓓ **infer**

5 I find *this* when I calculate the distance around a circle.
    Ⓐ **conference**   Ⓑ **chauffeur**   Ⓒ **referral**   Ⓓ **circumference**

6 Land that is *this* is richer and able to bear much vegetation.
    Ⓐ **referral**   Ⓑ **conference**   Ⓒ **prefer**   Ⓓ **fertile**

7 "Would you rather eat chicken nuggets or hamburgers for dinner?" "Which word below describes choosing hamburgers instead of chicken nuggets?"
    Ⓐ **referral**   Ⓑ **prefer**   Ⓒ **infer**   Ⓓ **offer**

8 Taylor, Tamara, and Chloe were going to *this* to hear new ideas on saving money.
    Ⓐ **conference**   Ⓑ **inference**   Ⓒ **referral**   Ⓓ **transfer**

9 Bob had to do *this* when the company he worked for decided to move from California to Kentucky.
    Ⓐ **differ**   Ⓑ **transfer**   Ⓒ **chauffeur**   Ⓓ **prefer**

10 When you have to "read between the lines" in a story to figure something out, you have to do *this* to reach a conclusion.
    Ⓐ **prefer**   Ⓑ **offer**   Ⓒ **infer**   Ⓓ **differ**

Write the correct word on the line so that the sentence makes sense and sounds grammatically correct.

11 Dominic and Matt _____ on where they thought their class should go on a field trip.

12 The soil was so _____ this year that the strawberry crop was twice the size as last year.

13 Judging by your comments and tone of voice, I can easily _____ that you are not happy with the vacation plans.

14 I do like macaroni and cheese, but I'd _____ to have chow mein for dinner this evening.

15 I'm going to have to _____ to another school when we move to Berea in March.

Review Test: tain, ten, tent, fer

Write the correct word from the word bank to complete each sentence.

1 I'd like to _____ an invitation to all of the eighth graders to join us at Hoyt Park for a graduation celebration.

2 We agree that the artwork should hang on the wall, but we _____ in our opinions of what colors to paint the artwork.

3 I need to measure the _____ of the table to make sure the glass top will fit before I purchase it.

4 Jeff was fortunate to have the same responsible _____ renting his lake cabin for the past seven years.

5 The witness to the accident _____ the driver until the police arrived.

6 I can _____ from the look on your face that you didn't like the taste of my new recipe for brussel sprouts.

7 The store was _____ a free set of sheets with every purchase of a down comforter.

8 Would you _____ to take surfing lessons or horseback riding lessons this summer?

9 After their son's many ear infections, the Phillips family was given a _____ to take him to a specialist.

10 "First, you'll need to take Bus #145 to the junction of Third and Pine. There, you'll need to _____ to Bus #450. You'll be in Yountville about 35 minutes later."

11 We made _____ plans to meet at 2:30 in front of the shopping center.

12 When inventing something new, it's important to file for a _____ to protect the ownership of your creation.

13 As a child, Laurie had hoped to have a _____ to drive her around when she became an adult.

14 At the medical _____, the doctors and nurses learned of new medical breakthroughs in the area of preventative medicine.

15 Sue's purse _____ so many things that the weight pulls down on her shoulder.

Word Bank
abstain
chauffeur
circumference
conference
contains
detained
detention
differ
extend
fertile
infer
offering
patent
prefer
referral
retainer
tenant
tendon
tentative
transfer

More Greek and Latin Roots • 4–8 © 2007 Creative Teaching Press

Word List: cap = take, seize

Vocabulary	Definitions
capable (adj)	having the ability; able to do something; able to **seize** an opportunity
capacity (n)	the ability to hold, **take** in, or absorb
capitalize (v)	to **take** advantage of something; to make the most of something
capsize (v)	to overturn; to **take** and flip over
caption (n)	a title or short description of a picture
capture (v)	to **take** possession or control of something; to **take** someone against his or her will; to preserve in a permanent form
decapitate (v)	to **take** the head off something
encapsulate (v)	to **take** in; to surround; to encase or protect
escape (v)	to **take** a path away; to leave; to get free
recapitulate (v)	to **take** the main ideas and repeat in a summarized form

More Greek and Latin Roots • 4–8 © 2007 Creative Teaching Press

Vocabulary Sort: cap

encapsulate	caption	capitalize	capacity	capsize
decapitate	escape	capable	capture	recapitulate

to **take** the main ideas and repeat in a summarized form	to **take** possession or control of something; to **take** someone against his or her will
to **take** the head off something	the ability to hold, **take** in, or absorb
having the ability; able to do something; able to **seize** an opportunity	to **take** in; to surround; to encase or protect
to overturn; to **take** and flip over	a title or short description of a picture
to **take** advantage of something; to make the most of something	to **take** a path away; to leave; to get free

More Greek and Latin Roots • 4–8 © 2007 Creative Teaching Press

Read-Around Review: cap

I have the first card.

Who has the root that means
to **take** or **seize**?

I have the root **cap**.

Who has the word that means
to surround or encase something?

I have the word **encapsulate**.

Who has the word that means
to **take** advantage of something,
such as an opportunity?

I have the word **capitalize**.

Who has the word that means
to **take** someone against his or her will?

I have the word **capture**.

Who has the word that means
a title or short description of a picture?

I have the word **caption**.

Who has the word that means
to leave or get away?

I have the word **escape**.

Who has the word that means
to summarize the main events
of a book or experience?

I have the word **recapitulate**.

Who has the word that means
to tip something over, such as
a canoe in the water?

I have the word **capsize**.

Who has the word that identifies how
much a container can hold?

I have the word **capacity**.

Who has the word that means a person
able to perform an action?

I have the word **capable**.

Who has the word that means
to remove the head of something?

I have the word **decapitate**.

Who has the first card?

Vocabulary Quiz: cap

Shade in the bubble for the correct word.

1. A new vacuum has *this*, or the ability to take in objects as heavy as a rock!
   - Ⓐ **capacity**
   - Ⓑ **capitalize**
   - Ⓒ **decapitate**
   - Ⓓ **recapitulate**

2. In ancient times, people were punished with this harsh method that is illegal today.
   - Ⓐ **decapitation**
   - Ⓑ **captivation**
   - Ⓒ **captioning**
   - Ⓓ **capability**

3. The milk chocolate coating on an ice-cream bar does *this* to the ice cream.
   - Ⓐ **captions**
   - Ⓑ **capsizes**
   - Ⓒ **recapitulates**
   - Ⓓ **encapsulates**

4. In nonfiction books, it is smart to read these short explanations for photos to help you clarify ideas.
   - Ⓐ **captions**
   - Ⓑ **capsizing**
   - Ⓒ **capabilities**
   - Ⓓ **decapitations**

5. The photographer tried to do *this* by seizing the joyful emotions of the moment within his images.
   - Ⓐ **escape**
   - Ⓑ **capture**
   - Ⓒ **capsize**
   - Ⓓ **decapitate**

6. After the raft flipped over, the swimmers returned to the shore. "What happened to their raft?"
   - Ⓐ **capsized**
   - Ⓑ **captured**
   - Ⓒ **recapitulated**
   - Ⓓ **capacity**

7. When a television personality suddenly achieves fame, he often tries to appear on magazine covers and talk shows to increase his popularity. "What is he doing with his fame?"
   - Ⓐ **capacity**
   - Ⓑ **capable**
   - Ⓒ **capitalizing**
   - Ⓓ **capsizing**

8. The teacher asked the students to write a summary for the first three chapters of their new novel. "What did they have to do with their ideas?"
   - Ⓐ **capture**
   - Ⓑ **recapitulate**
   - Ⓒ **escape**
   - Ⓓ **caption**

9. The ferret repeatedly tried to break out of its cage! "What was he trying to do?"
   - Ⓐ **escape**
   - Ⓑ **capture**
   - Ⓒ **capsize**
   - Ⓓ **capacity**

10. Sam is this type of person because she is able to achieve any realistic goal she sets for herself.
    - Ⓐ **escape**
    - Ⓑ **capsize**
    - Ⓒ **caption**
    - Ⓓ **capable**

Write the correct word on the line so that the sentence makes sense and sounds grammatically correct.

11. Most cartoons found in newspapers have a one-sentence _____ that enhances the ideas in the image.

12. Carlos' new sleeping bag is large enough to _____ himself and his two dogs!

13. Jim decided to _____ on his ability to sing by becoming the lead singer in a band.

14. Our new car has the _____ to hold five passengers and the driver.

15. Zookeepers tried to _____ the bear that escaped from its habitat.

More Greek and Latin Roots • 4–8 © 2007 Creative Teaching Press

Word List: pel, puls = drive, driven, force

Vocabulary	Definitions
compel (v)	to **force** someone to do something; to **drive** someone into action
dispel (v)	to **drive** away; to **force** out of one's mind; to go away
expel (v)	to **force** or **drive** out; to **force** to leave
impel (v)	to **drive** forward; to urge to action; to motivate
impulse (n)	a sudden urge that **drives** someone into action
propel (v)	to **force** to move forward; to **drive** onward
pulsate (v)	to vibrate; beat; **forced** to produce short bursts
repel (v)	to **drive** back; to ward off or keep away
repellent (n)	a substance used to **drive** away insects or animals
repulsive (adj)	disgusting; tending to **drive** off; offensive

More Greek and Latin Roots • 4–8 © 2007 Creative Teaching Press

Vocabulary Sort: pel, puls

impel	propel	pulsate	compel	repellent
repulsive	repel	impulse	expel	dispel

a substance used to **drive** away insects or animals	to **force** or **drive** out; to **force** to leave
a sudden urge that **drives** someone into action	disgusting; tending to **drive** off; offensive
to **drive** back; to ward off or keep away	to **force** someone to do something; to **drive** someone into action
to **drive** away; to **force** out of one's mind; to go away	to **force** to move forward; to **drive** onward
to vibrate; beat; **forced** to produce short bursts	to **drive** forward; to urge to action; to motivate

More Greek and Latin Roots • 4–8 © 2007 Creative Teaching Press

Read-Around Review: pel, puls

I have the first card. Who has the roots that mean to **drive**, **driven**, or **force**?	I have the word **impel**. Who has the word that means to **force** forward, as in throwing an object?
I have the roots **pel** and **puls**. Who has the word that means to vibrate or produce short bursts in a rhythmic motion?	I have the word **propel**. Who has the word that means to **drive** out or eliminate from a situation?
I have the word **pulsate**. Who has the word that means to ward off or keep something away, such as bugs or bees?	I have the word **expel**. Who has the word that means to **drive** someone into doing something?
I have the word **repel**. Who has the word that means to **drive** away or **force** to go away?	I have the word **compel**. Who has the word that identifies a substance, such as bug spray, used to **drive** off insects?
I have the word **dispel**. Who has the word that means a strong, sudden urge that **drives** someone to action?	I have the word **repellent**. Who has the word that means disgusting?
I have the word **impulse**. Who has the word that means to **drive** forward into an action or to motivate someone to take action?	I have the word **repulsive**. Who has the first card?

More Greek and Latin Roots • 4–8 © 2007 Creative Teaching Press

Name _____   Date _____

Vocabulary Quiz: pel, puls

Shade in the bubble for the correct word.

1. "You should forget all the rumors and only listen to the facts." "What should you do with the rumors?"
   - Ⓐ **dispel**
   - Ⓑ **repel**
   - Ⓒ **repellent**
   - Ⓓ **impulse**

2. *This* happened to the athlete when he was driven forward by a sudden burst of adrenaline.
   - Ⓐ **repelled**
   - Ⓑ **pulsated**
   - Ⓒ **expelled**
   - Ⓓ **propelled**

3. She could feel her heartbeat racing or *this* as she finished the marathon in record time.
   - Ⓐ **repulsive**
   - Ⓑ **pulsating**
   - Ⓒ **impel**
   - Ⓓ **repelled**

4. "That smell is so disgusting! What can it possibly be?" "What word below describes the awful smell?"
   - Ⓐ **repel**
   - Ⓑ **repulsive**
   - Ⓒ **impel**
   - Ⓓ **pulsating**

5. When camping, it is important to use bug spray to keep away biting insects. "What is another word that means to keep away?"
   - Ⓐ **repel**
   - Ⓑ **impel**
   - Ⓒ **compel**
   - Ⓓ **repulsive**

6. "I cannot emphasize enough how important it is for you to study and try your best." "What word below describes what this person is trying to do with his or her ideas?"
   - Ⓐ **impel**
   - Ⓑ **repel**
   - Ⓒ **pulsate**
   - Ⓓ **dispel**

7. The boy was kicked out of school for making poor choices. "What happened to him?"
   - Ⓐ **impelled**
   - Ⓑ **impulsive**
   - Ⓒ **compelled**
   - Ⓓ **expelled**

8. John had a sudden urge or *this* to eat ice cream, so he drove straight to the local ice cream shop.
   - Ⓐ **repulsive**
   - Ⓑ **impulse**
   - Ⓒ **pulsate**
   - Ⓓ **repellent**

9. She felt driven or *this* to choose Hawaii for her vacation destination.
   - Ⓐ **expelled**
   - Ⓑ **compelled**
   - Ⓒ **repelled**
   - Ⓓ **dispelled**

10. "There are so many mosquitoes outside today! What should I use to get rid of them?"
    - Ⓐ **repellent**
    - Ⓑ **impelled**
    - Ⓒ **compelled**
    - Ⓓ **impulsive**

Write the correct word on the line so that the sentence makes sense and sounds grammatically correct.

11. Although most people love tuna, I find the smell to be _____.

12. The green and yellow neon lights were _____ on the billboard!

13. It's important to _____ any negative thoughts from the mind and focus on only the positive thoughts.

14. Remember to pack some insect _____, so you won't be bitten while on the hike.

15. Sometimes she had the sudden _____ to go shopping at the mall, but she tried to overcome those urges to spend money.

50

More Greek and Latin Roots • 4–8 © 2007 Creative Teaching Press

Review Test: cap, pel, puls

Write the correct word from the word bank to complete each sentence.

1 She learned how to speak English by watching closed-_____ television, in which the spoken words that go along with the images are printed at the bottom of the television screen.

2 Luckily, they were all wearing life jackets when their rafts _____ while on the river rafting expedition.

3 Her heart was _____ so quickly after running up the steep hill that she had to sit down to rest.

4 She felt _____ to help the homeless man who was standing on the corner of the street by offering him a gift card to the local grocery store.

5 Every school has the right to _____ students for improper behavior.

6 The gas tanks on many large vehicles have the _____ to hold 30 gallons of gasoline.

7 The teacher decided to _____ on the fact that her class loved animals, so she brought in a few of her pets to visit when the class demonstrated outstanding behavior.

8 Many adventure stories involve the _____ of a main character and the eventual release as an outcome.

9 She was in terrific physical shape for the track meet, but drank her fitness water just to see if it might help _____ her forward even faster.

10 The joke was so funny that he couldn't resist the _____ to laugh!

11 The sporting goods store had insect _____ on sale, because it was mosquito season.

12 Many people find it very _____ when they see a person spit on the ground.

13 You are _____ of succeeding at anything you try if you set your mind to it.

14 On the back of this paper, please give a _____ of your favorite story. Remember to include all of the main events.

15 A cocoon will completely _____ the caterpillar while it's changing from a silkworm to a moth.

Word Bank:
capable
capacity
capitalize
capsized
captioned
capture
compelled
decapitate
dispel
encapsulate
escape
expel
impel
impulse
propel
pulsating
recapitulation
repel
repellent
repulsive

Word List: pend = hang, weigh, pay

Vocabulary	Definitions
appendix (n)	a collection of supplementary material that usually "**hangs**" at the end of a book; extra materials added to the end of a book
dependent (adj)	relying on someone else for aid or support; **weighing** down on someone else
expenditure (n)	an expense; the amount needed to be **paid** out
impending (adj)	about to occur; to threaten to happen; to **weigh** down upon someone
independent (adj)	not relying on someone else for aid or support; not **weighing** down on someone else
pendant (n)	an object that **hangs**, usually from a necklace
pending (adj)	**hanging** on; something not yet decided; awaiting a conclusion
pendulum (n)	something that **hangs** and swings back and forth
perpendicular (adj)	intersecting at or forming right angles
suspended (v)	**hanging**; delayed

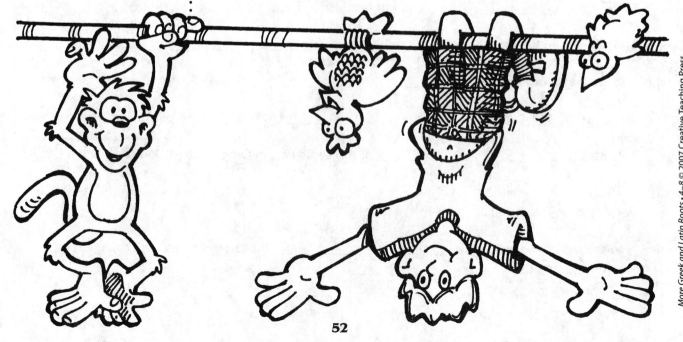

More Greek and Latin Roots • 4–8 © 2007 Creative Teaching Press

Vocabulary Sort: pend

dependent	independent	pending	pendulum	appendix
impending	perpendicular	suspended	pendant	expenditure

an object that **hangs**, usually from a necklace	**hanging**; delayed
an expense; the amount needed to be **paid** out	about to occur; to threaten to happen; to **weigh** down upon someone
something that **hangs** and swings back and forth	**hanging** on; something not yet decided; awaiting a conclusion
intersecting at or forming right angles	a collection of supplementary material that usually "**hangs**" at the end of a book; extra materials added to the end of the book
relying on someone else for aid or support; **weighing** down on someone else	not relying on someone else for aid or support; not **weighing** down on someone else

More Greek and Latin Roots • 4–8 © 2007 Creative Teaching Press

Read-Around Review: pend

I have the first card. Who has the root that means to **hang**, **weigh**, or **pay**?	I have the word **impending**. Who has the word that describes a person who relies only on himself or herself?
I have the root **pend**. Who has the word that identifies something **hanging** from a necklace?	I have the word **independent**. Who has the word that describes a person who relies on others rather than himself or herself?
I have the word **pendant**. Who has the word that means intersecting at or forming right angles?	I have the word **dependent**. Who has the word that means an expense, or money that was spent on something?
I have the word **perpendicular**. Who has the word that identifies the object that **hangs** and swings back and forth on a grandfather clock?	I have the word **expenditure**. Who has the word that describes a transaction that has not been concluded?
I have the word **pendulum**. Who has the word that describes **hanging** in midair?	I have the word **pending**. Who has the word that names the extra materials added to the back of some books?
I have the word **suspended**. Who has the word that describes something that is about to happen that could cause negative results?	I have the word **appendix**. Who has the first card?

More Greek and Latin Roots • 4–8 © 2007 Creative Teaching Press

Name _____ Date _____

Vocabulary Quiz: pend

Shade in the bubble for the correct word.

1 Sometimes magicians try to hypnotize someone with one of these objects as it sways back and forth.
Ⓐ **perpendicular**   Ⓑ **pendulum**   Ⓒ **expenditure**   Ⓓ **appendix**

2 Linda's admittance into college was *this* because the college hadn't received her final grades.
Ⓐ **pending**   Ⓑ **independent**   Ⓒ **pendant**   Ⓓ **expenditures**

3 The siren sounded in the town to warn people of the upcoming tornado. "What word below indicates that something was about to occur?"
Ⓐ **independent**   Ⓑ **impending**   Ⓒ **dependent**   Ⓓ **appendix**

4 Her great-grandmother's locket or *this* hung from the gold chain she wore every day.
Ⓐ **pendant**   Ⓑ **pendulum**   Ⓒ **perpendicular**   Ⓓ **impending**

5 Kim has been living alone for the past ten years, so she's used to taking care of herself. "What word below describes this type of person?"
Ⓐ **independent**   Ⓑ **dependent**   Ⓒ **expenditure**   Ⓓ **suspended**

6 If you are spending more money than you earn, you might have too many of *these*.
Ⓐ **expenditures**   Ⓑ **appendix**   Ⓒ **suspended**   Ⓓ **pendulum**

7 What word below describes people who need help from others?
Ⓐ **dependent**   Ⓑ **independent**   Ⓒ **pendants**   Ⓓ **expenditures**

8 Parallel lines are the opposite of these lines that intersect to create perfect right angles.
Ⓐ **impending**   Ⓑ **suspended**   Ⓒ **dependent**   Ⓓ **perpendicular**

9 The author included maps and character lists in this supplemental section of his book.
Ⓐ **pending**   Ⓑ **pendant**   Ⓒ **appendix**   Ⓓ **dependent**

10 What word below describes a spider web that is hanging between two trees?
Ⓐ **perpendicular**   Ⓑ **suspended**   Ⓒ **impending**   Ⓓ **pending**

Write the correct word on the line so that the sentence makes sense and sounds grammatically correct.

11 She was filled with _____ doom knowing that the hurricane was only moments away.

12 Walter's decision to purchase a new car was _____ because he had not yet seen the car's history report.

13 If you tie a spoon to a string and swing it back and forth, you will have created a _____.

14 Martha's _____ were so high that she needed to borrow money to pay for many things.

15 Zack had a hard time making decisions. He was very _____ upon his friends to make choices for him.

Word List: stat = stay, position, to know

Vocabulary	Definitions
ecstatic (adj)	extreme joy; **to know** the feeling of pure delight
estate (n)	a considerably large piece of property; high social **position** or rank; the whole of one's possessions
static (adj)	fixed; to **stay** with no motion; not active
station (n)	the place or **position** where a person or thing stands or is assigned to stand; a post
stationary (adj)	not moving; not capable of being moved; fixed in **position**
stature (n)	one's height in an upright **position**; an achieved **position** or level
status (n)	**position** in society relative to others
status quo (n)	**staying** the same; unchanging
statute (n)	a law; a rule created by someone of a high **position**
thermostat (n)	a device that responds to temperature changes in order to maintain its set **position**

More Greek and Latin Roots • 4–8 © 2007 Creative Teaching Press

Vocabulary Sort: stat

stationary	statute	thermostat	ecstatic	estate
station	status	static	stature	status quo

position in society relative to others	not moving; not capable of being moved; fixed in **position**
extreme joy; **to know** the feeling of pure delight	**staying** the same; unchanging
a law; a rule created by someone of a high **position**	one's height in an upright **position**; an achieved **position** or level
a considerably large piece of property; high social **position** or rank; the whole of one's possessions	fixed; to **stay** with no motion; not active
a device that responds to temperature changes in order to maintain its set **position**	the place or **position** where a person or thing stands or is assigned to stand; a post

More Greek and Latin Roots • 4–8 © 2007 Creative Teaching Press

Read-Around Review: stat

I have the first card. Who has the root that means **stay**, **position**, or **to know**?	I have the words **status quo**. Who has the word that names a law or rule that people must follow?
I have the root **stat**. Who has the word that describes something that is in a fixed **position** and unmoving?	I have the word **statute**. Who has the word that describes something that has no motion by itself?
I have the word **stationary**. Who has the word that means the way a person stands in an upright **position**?	I have the word **static**. Who has the word that describes a very excited and joyful person?
I have the word **stature**. Who has the word that names a person's worth or value as compared to others in society?	I have the word **ecstatic**. Who has the word that names a device used to keep the temperature in the same **position**?
I have the word **status**. Who has the word that names the place where a person is told to stand and work, such as the **position** of a store cashier?	I have the word **thermostat**. Who has the word that identifies all of the valuable property owned by a person?
I have the word **station**. Who has the words that identify a preference for keeping things the same?	I have the word **estate**. Who has the first card?

More Greek and Latin Roots • 4–8 © 2007 Creative Teaching Press

Vocabulary Quiz: stat

Shade in the bubble for the correct word.

1 The property included stables and a two-story guest house. "What word below describes this property?"
   Ⓐ status quo   Ⓑ statute   Ⓒ stature   Ⓓ estate

2 The built-in desk could not be removed. "What word below describes the placement of this desk?"
   Ⓐ stationary   Ⓑ status   Ⓒ ecstatic   Ⓓ statute

3 Emily's job was to stand at the window and announce when the birthday girl arrived to her surprise party. "What is another word for the place Emily was assigned to stand?"
   Ⓐ station   Ⓑ status quo   Ⓒ ecstatic   Ⓓ statue

4 Cristobal was told to practice walking while standing up straight to improve *this*.
   Ⓐ status   Ⓑ stature   Ⓒ statute   Ⓓ stationary

5 Tom has lived in the same apartment and driven the same car for over ten years. "What word or words below describe the state of Tom's life?"
   Ⓐ status   Ⓑ statutes   Ⓒ static   Ⓓ status quo

6 Erin was always cold, so she had to continually adjust *this* to keep her home warm.
   Ⓐ thermostat   Ⓑ static   Ⓒ ecstatic   Ⓓ statute

7 Many of *these* have a time limit in which a person can prepare a lawsuit against another person if the law is broken.
   Ⓐ stationary   Ⓑ statutes   Ⓒ status   Ⓓ estates

8 What word below describes the level of a person's position in society?
   Ⓐ status   Ⓑ stationary   Ⓒ statues   Ⓓ estates

9 Lisa was so thrilled that she nearly began crying! "What word below describes the feeling Lisa was having?"
   Ⓐ status   Ⓑ status quo   Ⓒ ecstatic   Ⓓ stature

10 What word below describes a painting that has no feeling of movement?
   Ⓐ static   Ⓑ ecstatic   Ⓒ thermostat   Ⓓ station

Write the correct word on the line so that the sentence makes sense and sounds grammatically correct.

11 If you'd like to walk over to the salad _____, you can choose from among ten different items.

12 Some people buy expensive cars because they view them as _____ symbols.

13 While on vacation, Lucas visited the former _____ of the wealthy Rockefeller family.

14 Miles was so _____ when he found out he won the lottery!

15 Some people prefer to maintain the predictable _____, while others thrive on change in their lives.

More Greek and Latin Roots • 4–8 © 2007 Creative Teaching Press

Name _____   Date _____

Review Test: pend, stat

Write the correct word from the word bank to complete each sentence.

1 Where did you find that beautiful _____ hanging from your necklace?

2 They tried to adjust the temperature, but the _____ maintained the preset temperature.

3 She tried to make sure that her _____ did not exceed her income.

4 Kelli rushed to the grocery store to stock up on basic food items before the _____ storm arrived and washed out the roads.

5 Ms. May was truly gifted at helping her first graders become _____ readers and writers. They didn't ask their teacher for help at all!

6 The decision about whether or not Webster would get a promotion within his company was _____ while his boss awaited the results of his ability test.

7 If you want to know the laws in your city, you can find the _____ with a simple Internet search.

8 Some people prefer to ride a _____ bike at the gym so they do not have to ride on busy streets.

9 The newborns of most living creatures are _____ upon their mothers for nourishment.

10 I've never been so _____ in my life! I just won a two-week vacation to the Amazon rain forest!

11 The value of the _____ was estimated to be worth over $5 million.

12 Watching the swinging motion of a _____ is thought to make a person become sleepy.

13 The helicopter appeared to be _____ in midair! How in the world does it hover in one place like that?

14 The food at the wedding reception was organized into four _____ according to the countries they originated from.

15 Some people like things to stay the same. This means they like things as is, or _____.

Word Bank
appendix
dependent
ecstatic
estate
expenditures
impending
independent
pendant
pending
pendulum
perpendicular
static
stationary
stations
stature
status
status quo
statutes
suspended
thermostat

More Greek and Latin Roots • 4–8 © 2007 Creative Teaching Press

Word List: cogn, sci = to know, knowledge

Vocabulary	Definitions
cognition (n)	the mental process of **knowing**
cognizant (adj)	fully informed; **to know** or to be aware
conscience (n)	a source of moral or ethical judgment; **knowing** right from wrong
conscientious (adj)	thorough; principled; characterized by extreme care and effort
incognito (adj, adv)	describes an **unknown** identity; identity concealed
omniscient (adj)	having total **knowledge**; all **knowing**
recognize (v)	to identify or **know** someone; **to know** from past experience
scientist (n)	a person having expert **knowledge** in science
sciolistic (adj)	showing frivolous or superficial interest; amateur-like; superficial **knowledge** of something
unconscionable (adj)	unscrupulous; not restrained by the conscience; unreasonably unfair

More Greek and Latin Roots • 4–8 © 2007 Creative Teaching Press

Vocabulary Sort: cogn, sci

recognize	incognito	conscience	cognizant	scientist
sciolistic	unconscionable	cognition	conscientious	omniscient

describes an **unknown** identity; identity concealed	unscrupulous; not restrained by the conscience; unreasonably unfair
the mental process of **knowing**	fully informed; **to know** or to be aware
a person having expert **knowledge** in science	having total **knowledge**; all **knowing**
thorough; principled; characterized by extreme care and effort	to identify or **know** someone; **to know** from past experience
showing frivolous or superficial interest; amateur like; superficial **knowledge** of something	a source of moral or ethical judgment; **knowing** right from wrong

More Greek and Latin Roots • 4–8 © 2007 Creative Teaching Press

Read-Around Review: cogn, sci

I have the first card.

Who has the roots that mean **to know** or **knowledge**?

I have the roots **cogn, sci**.

Who has the word that identifies a person who is an expert in science?

I have the word **scientist**.

Who has the word that describes a person who says they have **knowledge** about a subject, but it is only superficial, not deep?

I have the word **sciolistic**.

Who has the word that describes someone who is able **to know** everything?

I have the word **omniscient**.

Who has the word that describes a person hiding his or her identity?

I have the word **incognito**.

Who has the word that describes the part of a person's mind that helps him determine right from wrong?

I have the word **conscience**.

Who has the word that describes what you are if you are fully aware of something going on around you?

I have the word **cognizant**.

Who has the word that describes an unbelievably cruel action that didn't involve good choices?

I have the word **unconscionable**.

Who has the word that means **to know** someone from a past experience, often because he or she looks familiar?

I have the word **recognize**.

Who has the word that means the mental process of **knowing**?

I have the word **cognition**.

Who has the word that describes people who are careful and thoughtful before taking action?

I have the word **conscientious**.

Who has the first card?

Name _____ Date _____

Vocabulary Quiz: cogn, sci

Shade in the bubble for the correct word.

1. "I know I've seen him somewhere, but I simply cannot remember his name!" "What is this person able to do?"
   Ⓐ **recognize**　　Ⓑ **conscience**　　Ⓒ **cognizant**　　Ⓓ **conscientious**

2. Before making her decision, Allie weighed the consequences. "What helped Allie make her decision?"
   Ⓐ **sciolistic**　　Ⓑ **unconscionable**　　Ⓒ **conscience**　　Ⓓ **incognito**

3. The actress wore a disguise so she wouldn't be recognized by her fans while on vacation. "What did the actress want to be?"
   Ⓐ **scientist**　　Ⓑ **unconscionable**　　Ⓒ **incognito**　　Ⓓ **cognizant**

4. In many fables and folktales, an owl is considered to be very wise and all-knowing or *this*.
   Ⓐ **omniscient**　　Ⓑ **scientist**　　Ⓒ **sciolistic**　　Ⓓ **conscience**

5. Dr. Vu is an expert in nutrients for the body. "What is his occupation?"
   Ⓐ **conscientious**　　Ⓑ **sciolistic**　　Ⓒ **cognizant**　　Ⓓ **scientist**

6. Villains in movies, television shows, and books often perform evil deeds toward other characters. "What word below describes these deeds?"
   Ⓐ **unconscionable**　　Ⓑ **recognize**　　Ⓒ **conscientious**　　Ⓓ **omniscient**

7. Principal Lopez was *this* because he was fully aware of what all of his students were doing at all times.
   Ⓐ **recognize**　　Ⓑ **incognito**　　Ⓒ **cognizant**　　Ⓓ **unconscionable**

8. What word below describes students who dedicate a great deal of time to being careful and hardworking?
   Ⓐ **scientist**　　Ⓑ **recognize**　　Ⓒ **cognition**　　Ⓓ **conscientious**

9. Ms. Itaya was studying *this* branch of psychology that focused on the mental process of knowing.
   Ⓐ **cognition**　　Ⓑ **sciolistic**　　Ⓒ **cognizant**　　Ⓓ **omniscient**

10. In order to become a lawyer, the man pretended to know every law. However, he was quickly proven to be a fraud with only minimal knowledge of the law. "What word below describes this type of knowledge?"
    Ⓐ **recognize**　　Ⓑ **omniscient**　　Ⓒ **conscientious**　　Ⓓ **sciolistic**

Write the correct word on the line so that the sentence makes sense and sounds grammatically correct.

11. Honest people consider what their _____ is telling them before making decisions.

12. It was hard to _____ her after she cut her hair and dyed it from blonde to black.

13. It was so _____ for him to trip that boy on the playground that he was immediately sent to speak with the principal.

14. The mysterious visitor seemed to have all of the answers. Everyone in town believed he was _____.

15. Ashleigh was such a _____ student that she studied for tests even when they were not announced.

More Greek and Latin Roots • 4–8 © 2007 Creative Teaching Press

Word List: sens, sent = feel, be aware

Vocabulary	Definitions
assenter (n)	a person who agrees or **feels** the same way
consensus (n)	an opinion or position agreed upon by a group; having a similar **feeling** or belief as others in a group
desensitize (v)	to lessen the **feeling** or **awareness**; to make less sensitive
dissent (v)	to differ in opinion or **feeling**; to disagree
nonsense (n)	of little importance; ridiculous; unimportant
resent (v)	to **feel** bitter or upset
sensational (adj)	outstanding; spectacular; **feelings** of success
sensible (adj)	showing reason or good judgment; able to **feel** or perceive
sensitive (adj)	**aware** of or affected by the attitudes, **feelings**, or circumstances of others
sentimental (adj)	having **feelings** of nostalgia; **feeling** that a thing is special because of how it relates to the past

Vocabulary Sort: sens, sent

sensible	sensational	dissent	assenter	sentimental
sensitive	nonsense	desensitize	consensus	resent

having **feelings** of nostalgia; **feeling** that a thing is special because of how it relates to the past	**aware** of or affected by the attitudes, **feelings**, or circumstances of others
of little importance; ridiculous; unimportant	to **feel** bitter or upset
a person who agrees or **feels** the same way	an opinion or position agreed upon by a group; having a similar **feeling** or belief as others in a group
showing reason or good judgment; able to **feel** or perceive	outstanding; spectacular; **feelings** of success
to lessen the **feeling** or **awareness**; to make less sensitive	to differ in opinion or **feeling**; to disagree

More Greek and Latin Roots • 4–8 © 2007 Creative Teaching Press

Read-Around Review: sens, sent

I have the first card. Who has the roots that mean to **feel** or to **be aware**?	I have the word **assenter**. Who has the word that describes a person who is **aware** of or affected by the actions, situations, or **feelings** of others?
I have the roots **sens** and **sent**. Who has the word that describes what you do if you disagree with someone?	I have the word **sensitive**. Who has the word that describes something that is fantastic?
I have the word **dissent**. Who has the word that describes a good choice that seems reasonable?	I have the word **sensational**. Who has the word that means that you are bitter and upset over something, such as an unfair decision?
I have the word **sensible**. Who has the word that means to lessen the **feeling** of something by being less sensitive to it, as in the case of an allergy?	I have the word **resent**. Who has the word that means something that is unimportant and often viewed as ridiculous?
I have the word **desensitize**. Who has the word that names what is reached when people in a group agree on a decision?	I have the word **nonsense**. Who has the word that describes a person who has strong **feelings** that remind the person of the past?
I have the word **consensus**. Who has the word that names a person who agrees with someone else?	I have the word **sentimental**. Who has the first card?

More Greek and Latin Roots • 4–8 © 2007 Creative Teaching Press

Name _____ Date _____

Vocabulary Quiz: sens, sent

Shade in the bubble for the correct word.

1 Damian didn't agree with his classmates when they voted on the location for the class celebration. "Which word below describes what Damian did?"
    Ⓐ **assenter**   Ⓑ **dissented**   Ⓒ **sensational**   Ⓓ **consensus**

2 She was so affected by movies that she cried at almost any film. "What word below describes this person?"
    Ⓐ **sensational**   Ⓑ **consensus**   Ⓒ **sensible**   Ⓓ **sensitive**

3 "You should feel very proud of the fantastic speech you delivered!" "What word describes the speech?"
    Ⓐ **sensible**   Ⓑ **resentful**   Ⓒ **sensational**   Ⓓ **desensitized**

4 Repeated exposures to something a person is allergic to will do *this* to them.
    Ⓐ **dissent**   Ⓑ **resentment**   Ⓒ **nonsense**   Ⓓ **desensitize**

5 "That seems like a reasonable decision," said Ms. Karian. "What word below is another word for reasonable?"
    Ⓐ **sensible**   Ⓑ **nonsense**   Ⓒ **resentful**   Ⓓ **sensational**

6 Nancy kept all of her childhood toys, books, and awards because they held special memories. "What word below describes Nancy?"
    Ⓐ **sensitive**   Ⓑ **desensitized**   Ⓒ **resentful**   Ⓓ **sentimental**

7 Nigel's comment to Paul was unkind and hurtful. "How was Paul feeling?"
    Ⓐ **resentful**   Ⓑ **sensational**   Ⓒ **desensitized**   Ⓓ **assented**

8 "That's the most ridiculous thing that I've ever heard! You can't create wings that will make you fly!" "What word below describes this idea?"
    Ⓐ **resentment**   Ⓑ **assenting**   Ⓒ **sentimental**   Ⓓ **nonsense**

9 Every member of the group agreed to the change. "What word below describes the group's decision?"
    Ⓐ **dissent**   Ⓑ **assenter**   Ⓒ **consensus**   Ⓓ **sensitive**

10 What word below describes a person who always goes along with what everyone else in the group says?
    Ⓐ **assenter**   Ⓑ **dissenter**   Ⓒ **resentment**   Ⓓ **sentimentalist**

Write the correct word on the line so that the sentence makes sense and sounds grammatically correct.

11 The hard-working man tried not to _____ his boss when he was not given the promotion.

12 "I find that hard to believe. It sounds like utter _____ to me."

13 "Let's try to be _____ about this. You simply cannot have twelve rabbits as pets!"

14 The group reached _____ and agreed to invite Jan to join the club.

15 *Assenter* is to *agrees* as _____ is to *disagrees*.

More Greek and Latin Roots • 4–8 © 2007 Creative Teaching Press

Name _____ Date _____

Review Test: cogn, sci, sens, sent

Write the correct word from the word bank to complete each sentence.

1 Have you ever noticed how Ben always wants to do the exact opposite of everyone else? He's such a _____!

2 Abby said, "I wouldn't have recommended that book if I'd known how _____ you are. I didn't mean to make you cry for three days!"

3 Did you see the size of her sunglasses? Did she really think we wouldn't recognize her? She can try to go _____, but it'll never work!

4 Many people feel that doctors are _____, but most doctors openly admit that they are still learning, just like everyone else. They don't know everything!

5 Employees who are _____ are good role models.

6 There is a famous saying, "Let your _____ be your guide." That means to let your sense of right and wrong tell you what to do when facing a difficult decision.

7 The child had difficulty being in bright sunlight due to a rare illness. The doctors tried to _____ her to the light so that she could live a relatively normal life.

8 Did the members of the group ever reach _____? The last I heard, the vote was evenly split.

9 Many people feel that it was _____ for the Big Bad Wolf to impersonate the grandma to get Little Red Riding Hood. How dare he!

10 Her decision still bothers me so much that I can't help but _____ her.

11 I don't remember how to get there, but when I see the building I'll surely _____ it.

12 He was _____ of the fact that everyone in the room was cheering him on in the National Spelling Bee.

13 I know it sounds like _____, but it's very important to me.

14 Chemists, biologists, and pharmacists are all specific examples of _____.

15 Her portable music system was filled with old songs that reminded her of past experiences. She was so _____.

assenter
cognition
cognizant
conscience
conscientious
consensus
desensitize
dissenter
incognito
nonsense
omniscient
recognize
resent
scientists
sciolistic
sensational
sensible
sensitive
sentimental
unconscionable

Word List: duc, duct = lead, take, bring

Vocabulary	Definitions
abduct (v)	to **lead** away by force; to kidnap
aqueduct (n)	a channel that **brings** water from a remote source
conducive (adj)	tending to cause or **bring** about
deduce (v)	to reach a conclusion by reasoning; to infer; to **lead** to a conclusion
deductible (n)	the amount that will be **taken** out first; the payment owed before an expense is covered by insurance
deduction (n)	the amount that must be **taken** out; subtraction
introduce (v)	to **bring** into a group; to meet
introduction (n)	the section that **leads** into a book; the opening
produce (v)	to **bring** forth
reduce (v)	to **take** down to a smaller form; to **bring** down

More Greek and Latin Roots • 4–8 © 2007 Creative Teaching Press

Vocabulary Sort: duc, duct

conducive	introduce	abduct	reduce	aqueduct
introduction	deduce	produce	deductible	deduction

the amount that must be **taken** out; subtraction	a channel that **brings** water from a remote source
to **take** down to a smaller form; to **bring** down	to **bring** forth
to **lead** away by force; to kidnap	tending to cause or **bring** about
to reach a conclusion by reasoning; to infer; to **lead** to a conclusion	the amount that will be **taken** out first; the payment owed before an expense is covered by insurance
the section that **leads** into a book; the opening	to **bring** into a group; to meet

Read-Around Review: duc, duct

I have the first card.

Who has the roots that mean
to **lead**, **take**, or **bring**?

I have the word **deduction**.

Who has the word that describes
what you are doing when you make
something smaller?

I have the roots **duc** and **duct**.

Who has the word that identifies the
beginning section of a book?

I have the word **reduce**.

Who has the word that means
to force another person to leave
against his or her will?

I have the word **introduction**.

Who has the word that means likely to
cause or **bring** about something?

I have the word **abduct**.

Who has the word that describes
what you are doing when you
create something?

I have the word **conducive**.

Who has the word that identifies
the amount of money that must be paid
before insurance will cover an expense?

I have the word **produce**.

Who has the word that identifies the
channel that often **brings** water from a
remote source to a water reservoir?

I have the word **deductible**.

Who has the word that describes
bringing a person into a group so he or
she can meet the other members?

I have the word **aqueduct**.

Who has the word that means to figure
something out or make an inference?

I have the word **introduce**.

Who has the word that names
the amount of money **taken** out of
a bank account?

I have the word **deduce**.

Who has the first card?

More Greek and Latin Roots • 4–8 © 2007 Creative Teaching Press

Name _____ Date _____

Vocabulary Quiz: duc, duct

Shade in the bubble for the correct word.

1 Information on the detective's past cases was presented in this section of the book.
Ⓐ **produced**   Ⓑ **deductible**   Ⓒ **reduction**   Ⓓ **introduction**

2 Before Ann's insurance would pay for her injury, she had to pay a specific amount, or *this* first.
Ⓐ **introduction**   Ⓑ **deductible**   Ⓒ **production**   Ⓓ **reduction**

3 To do *this* to a fraction, simplify it by dividing the numerator and denominator by the same number.
Ⓐ **reduce**   Ⓑ **produce**   Ⓒ **deduce**   Ⓓ **abduct**

4 The girl had been missing for two hours. Her parents began to worry that someone had done *this* to her.
Ⓐ **production**   Ⓑ **aqueduct**   Ⓒ **abducted**   Ⓓ **deduction**

5 It is polite to do *this* with people who have not met before.
Ⓐ **produce**   Ⓑ **reduce**   Ⓒ **deduce**   Ⓓ **introduce**

6 After three years of film school, the two friends were thrilled to be creating their first screenplay together. "What word below means *to create*?"
Ⓐ **reduce**   Ⓑ **produce**   Ⓒ **deduce**   Ⓓ **abduct**

7 What word describes the money people can subtract from their income taxes when they donate to charity?
Ⓐ **deduction**   Ⓑ **abduction**   Ⓒ **deductible**   Ⓓ **production**

8 What word below describes how the person figured out the answer to the riddle?
Ⓐ **reduce**   Ⓑ **introduce**   Ⓒ **produce**   Ⓓ **deduce**

9 The classroom was so disorderly and filthy that it wasn't an appropriate learning environment. "This room is *not* what?"
Ⓐ **conducive**   Ⓑ **produced**   Ⓒ **abducted**   Ⓓ **introduced**

10 This type of channel brings water from rainy Northern California to dry Southern California.
Ⓐ **aqueduct**   Ⓑ **product**   Ⓒ **deduction**   Ⓓ **deductible**

Write the correct word on the line so that the sentence makes sense and sounds grammatically correct.

11 The toys all over the floor were not _____ to the toddler learning to walk for the first time.

12 The dancers who were to perform in the ballet were _____ by name in alphabetical order prior to the show.

13 Lucy needed to make a _____ from her bank account to pay for her new necklace.

14 The new pineapple plantation is hoping to _____ 50 tons of pineapples each year.

15 Based on the clues revealed, I _____ that the maid is the guilty party.

More Greek and Latin Roots • 4–8 © 2007 Creative Teaching Press

Word List: flu, flux = to flow

Vocabulary	Definitions
affluence (n)	a plentiful supply; wealth; a great quantity that seems to keep **flowing**
confluence (n)	a gathering, meeting, or **flowing** together at one point; a joining
effluence (n)	something that **flows** out; outflow
fluctuate (v)	to rise and fall irregularly; to vary; **to flow** up and down unpredictably
fluent (adj)	able **to flow** smoothly; graceful
fluid (n)	a substance whose molecules **flow** freely past one another; a liquid or gas
fluted (adj)	a tall, narrow shape designed for a smooth **flow** of liquid
influential (adj)	having the power to make things **flow** their way; the **flow** of power
influx (n)	a **flowing** in of something in a large number or amount; a mass arrival
superfluous (adj)	**overflow**; more than enough; an overabundance; more than required

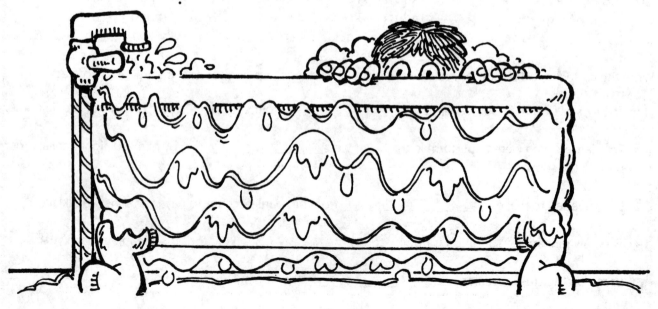

More Greek and Latin Roots · 4–8 © 2007 Creative Teaching Press

Vocabulary Sort: flu, flux

influential	fluted	effluence	affluence	superfluous
influx	fluid	fluctuate	confluence	fluent

able **to flow** smoothly; graceful	**overflow**; more than enough; an overabundance; more than required
a **flowing** in of something in a large number or amount; a mass arrival	a substance whose molecules **flow** freely past one another; a liquid or gas
a plentiful supply; wealth; a great quantity that seems to keep **flowing**	a gathering, meeting, or **flowing** together at one point; a joining
a tall, narrow shape designed for a smooth **flow** of liquid	having the power to make things **flow** their way; the **flow** of power
something that **flows** out; outflow	to rise and fall irregularly; to vary; **to flow** up and down unpredictably

Read-Around Review: flu, flux

I have the first card. Who has the roots that mean **to flow**?	I have the word **effluence**. Who has the word that describes when a person reads smoothly, like in natural speech?
I have the roots **flu** and **flux**. Who has the word that describes what a person is when he or she can get what they want out of someone else?	I have the word **fluent**. Who has the word that means that a person has a plentiful supply of wealth?
I have the word **influential**. Who has the word that describes what is happening when something, such as the temperature, moves up and down?	I have the word **affluence**. Who has the word that identifies a liquid or gas that **flows** smoothly?
I have the word **fluctuates**. Who has the word that describes the shape of a glass designed to create a certain **flow** of the liquid placed within?	I have the word **fluid**. Who has the word that identifies a large number of things, such as a huge swarm of bees, entering an area?
I have the word **fluted**. Who has the word that describes having more than necessary?	I have the word **influx**. Who has the word that means a gathering or meeting together at one point?
I have the word **superfluous**. Who has the word that means something that **flows** out?	I have the word **confluence**. Who has the first card?

More Greek and Latin Roots • 4–8 © 2007 Creative Teaching Press

Vocabulary Quiz: flu, flux

Shade in the bubble for the correct word.

1. By using this shape of a glass instead of a wide, short glass, you'll be able to see water pour out smoothly.
   Ⓐ **fluent**   Ⓑ **fluted**   Ⓒ **influential**   Ⓓ **confluence**

2. Because of the sudden arrival or *this* of so many mosquitoes, the stores ran out of insect repellant.
   Ⓐ **influx**   Ⓑ **affluence**   Ⓒ **influential**   Ⓓ **superfluous**

3. Flowing lava molecules have the ability to move freely past each other because they are *this*.
   Ⓐ **superfluous**   Ⓑ **fluctuate**   Ⓒ **influential**   Ⓓ **fluid**

4. What word describes more than enough books donated to the shelter?
   Ⓐ **superfluous**   Ⓑ **fluctuate**   Ⓒ **affluence**   Ⓓ **fluid**

5. Luca could speak and understand the Spanish language clearly. "What word below describes Luca's use of Spanish?"
   Ⓐ **affluence**   Ⓑ **confluence**   Ⓒ **fluent**   Ⓓ **influx**

6. What word below describes a person who has made a difference in someone else's life?
   Ⓐ **confluence**   Ⓑ **effluence**   Ⓒ **influential**   Ⓓ **fluted**

7. Mark was upset and couldn't stop his emotions from flowing. "What word describes his outpour of emotions?"
   Ⓐ **affluent**   Ⓑ **effluence**   Ⓒ **influence**   Ⓓ **influx**

8. The values of public corporations traded on the stock market do *this* because they vary every minute.
   Ⓐ **influx**   Ⓑ **fluctuate**   Ⓒ **confluence**   Ⓓ **effluence**

9. Many people mistakenly wish for more money or *this* when what they truly desire is more happiness.
   Ⓐ **affluence**   Ⓑ **fluctuate**   Ⓒ **influx**   Ⓓ **effluence**

10. The visitors wanted to take photos of this mass meeting of swallows at the local mission.
    Ⓐ **confluence**   Ⓑ **fluent**   Ⓒ **effluence**   Ⓓ **superfluous**

Write the correct word on the line so that the sentence makes sense and sounds grammatically correct.

11. Most substances that are _____ at room temperature will become solid when placed in freezing temperatures.

12. As a result of the _____ of young families in the community, the school was able to open three additional kindergarten classrooms.

13. Many mathematicians name Albert Einstein as being _____ in their studies.

14. It's better for your bank account to steadily grow in size rather than _____ from month to month.

15. Every winter when monarchs migrate south, there is a _____ of butterflies in Mexico.

More Greek and Latin Roots • 4–8 © 2007 Creative Teaching Press

Review Test: duc, duct, flu, flux

Write the correct word from the word bank to complete each sentence.

1 Brenda decided that she needed to _____ her workload, because she never had time to just enjoy being with her family.

2 As a trilingual translator, Miguel was _____ in English, Spanish, and Cantonese.

3 The university was surprised by the _____ of students who wanted to study economics. It was the most in a single year that the college had ever seen.

4 Magazines can be very _____ in the lives of young people; however, teens need to understand that some images and stories are fictional and published for publicity purposes.

5 Carmela doesn't like it when the temperature _____. She prefers the temperature to remain constant.

6 The presentation began after the _____ of the guest speaker.

7 Being in a room with people who wear a great deal of perfume is not _____ to a person who has severe allergies.

8 Judging by her wardrobe, one might _____ that she is very wealthy.

9 She paid the $250.00 _____ first, and then the insurance company paid for the rest of her hospital expenses.

10 From 2004–2005, the company _____ 7.6 million tons of buttons.

11 "Ladies and gentlemen, I'd like to _____ our guest speaker for the evening."

12 Within a week, Quincy made three _____ from the bank using his ATM card.

13 I think if you are a person with _____, you should donate money to charities.

14 The popular motorcycle club gathers in the same place once a year. This _____ is a sight to see!

15 A _____ amount of crayons was delivered to the school, so some were donated to the local homeless shelter.

Word Bank

abduct
affluence
aqueduct
conducive
confluence
deduce
deductible
deductions
effluence
fluctuates
fluent
fluid
fluted
influential
influx
introduce
introduction
produced
reduce
superfluous

More Greek and Latin Roots • 4–8 © 2007 Creative Teaching Press

Word List: aud, son, phon = sound, to hear

Vocabulary	Definitions
assonance (n)	the repetition of similar vowel **sounds** in the stressed syllables of successive words
audible (adj)	able to be **heard**
audio (n)	the **sound** portion of a broadcast
auditorium (n)	a large room that accommodates an audience, often for meetings or performances
cacophony (n)	harsh **sounds**; noisy or disturbing **sounds**
phonograph (n)	a record player; a machine that reproduces **sound**
resonate (v)	to vibrate or repeat in **sound**; to correspond harmoniously
sonar (n)	echolocation; a system using transmitted and reflected underwater **sound** waves to detect and locate submerged objects
sonnet (n)	a poem with 14 lines that usually **sounds** like one of several conventional rhyme schemes
unison (n)	words or music produced by more than one person that **sounds** as if from one voice

More Greek and Latin Roots • 4–8 © 2007 Creative Teaching Press

Vocabulary Sort: aud, son, phon

cacophony	unison	sonar	audible	sonnet
assonance	audio	phonograph	auditorium	resonate

harsh **sounds**; noisy or disturbing **sounds**	a record player; a machine that reproduces **sound**
a large room that accommodates an audience, often for meetings or performances	words or music produced by more than one person that **sounds** as if from one voice
to vibrate or repeat in **sound**; to correspond harmoniously	able to be **heard**
the repetition of similar vowel **sounds** in the stressed syllables of successive words	a poem with 14 lines that usually **sounds** like one of several conventional rhyme schemes
echolocation; a system using transmitted and reflected underwater **sound** waves to detect and locate submerged objects	the **sound** portion of a broadcast

More Greek and Latin Roots • 4–8 © 2007 Creative Teaching Press

Read-Around Review: aud, son, phon

I have the first card.

Who has the roots that mean
sound or **to hear**?

I have the word **phonograph**.

Who has the word that describes
the **sound** portion of a television
program or movie?

I have the roots **aud**, **son**, and **phon**.

Who has the word that names the method
used by submarines to maneuver within
the ocean by using sound waves?

I have the word **audio**.

Who has the word that describes
something that is within your
range of **hearing**?

I have the word **sonar**.

Who has the word that identifies
a type of poetry in which the lines **sound**
like specific rhyming styles?

I have the word **audible**.

Who has the word that names the room
where people go to see a performance,
such as the play *Peter and the Wolf*?

I have the word **sonnet**.

Who has the word that describes
a loud and often disturbing **sound**?

I have the word **auditorium**.

Who has the word that identifies a string
of words that use similar **sounds**?

I have the word **cacophony**.

Who has the word that names how a group
of people **sound** when they are all singing
together as if they were one person?

I have the word **assonance**.

Who has the word that means
to vibrate or repeat a **sound**, often
in a harmonious way?

I have the word **unison**.

Who has the word that identifies
the device that reproduces **sound**
(also known as a record player)?

I have the word **resonate**.

Who has the first card?

More Greek and Latin Roots • 4–8 © 2007 Creative Teaching Press

Name _____   Date _____

Vocabulary Quiz: aud, son, phon

Shade in the bubble for the correct word.

1 Although three people were singing, it sounded like one beautiful voice because the group was singing in *this*.
Ⓐ **sonnet**　　Ⓑ **cacophony**　　Ⓒ **unison**　　Ⓓ **assonance**

2 According to many wildlife advocates, the use of this underwater system is actually dangerous to whales.
Ⓐ **sonar**　　Ⓑ **assonance**　　Ⓒ **resonates**　　Ⓓ **sonnets**

3 Her kind words seem to vibrate, or do *this*, in my ears.
Ⓐ **resonate**　　Ⓑ **audible**　　Ⓒ **cacophonic**　　Ⓓ **audio**

4 The presenter used a microphone so that her speech would be *this*.
Ⓐ **resonate**　　Ⓑ **cacophony**　　Ⓒ **assonance**　　Ⓓ **audible**

5 Most children today don't know what one of these devices was created to do, because they've grown up in the age of CD and MP3 players.
Ⓐ **sonnet**　　Ⓑ **phonograph**　　Ⓒ **cacophony**　　Ⓓ **auditorium**

6 The audience was seated in this room of the building awaiting the start of the famous dance troupe.
Ⓐ **auditorium**　　Ⓑ **phonograph**　　Ⓒ **sonnet**　　Ⓓ **assonance**

7 The crows were making so much noise that the guests couldn't hear what the tour guide was announcing. "What word below describes the crows' noise?"
Ⓐ **assonance**　　Ⓑ **unison**　　Ⓒ **resonate**　　Ⓓ **cacophony**

8 One of the most famous examples of *this* is: "The rain in Spain falls mainly on the plain."
Ⓐ **sonnet**　　Ⓑ **unison**　　Ⓒ **cacophony**　　Ⓓ **assonance**

9 Kelly paid an extra $10.00 for *this* so she could hear the taped version of the museum tour.
Ⓐ **audio**　　Ⓑ **resonate**　　Ⓒ **sonar**　　Ⓓ **audible**

10 William Shakespeare is famous for writing more than 100 of these 14-line poems.
Ⓐ **assonance**　　Ⓑ **resonates**　　Ⓒ **cacophonies**　　Ⓓ **sonnets**

Write the correct word on the line so that the sentence makes sense and sounds grammatically correct.

11 Would someone please get her a microphone? Her speech is barely _____.

12 His writing assignment was to create an original 14-line _____ about his life.

13 The Five Browns are famous for their ability to play their pianos in _____, as if there was only one piano.

14 My mom still has her original records and _____ from her childhood.

15 *Euphonic* means beautiful in sound. The opposite of *euphonic* is _____.

More Greek and Latin Roots • 4–8 © 2007 Creative Teaching Press

Word List: tact, tang, tag, tig = touch

Vocabulary	Definitions
contact (n)	state or condition of **touching**
contagious (adj)	capable of transmitting an illness, infection, or disease by **touch**
contiguous (adj)	adjacent; **touching**; sharing an edge or boundary
entangle (v)	to twist together; making it complicated to free two things from **touching**
intact (adj)	whole; not damaged by **touch**
tactile (adj)	perceptible to the **touch**; used for feeling
tangent (n)	**touching** at a single point but not intersecting; a sudden digression or change of topic within a conversation; no longer **touching** on the subject
tangible (adj)	able to be **touched**
tangled (adj)	**touching** in a snarl; connected together in a disorderly way
tangy (adj)	a sharp taste or flavor immediately sensed upon **touch** with the tongue

Vocabulary Sort: tact, tang, tag, tig

tangible	entangle	contagious	contact	tangent
tangy	tangled	intact	tactile	contiguous

state or condition of **touching**	perceptible to the **touch**; used for feeling
whole; not damaged by **touch**	a sharp taste or flavor immediately sensed upon **touch** with the tongue
able to be **touched**	capable of transmitting an illness, infection, or disease by **touch**
touching in a snarl; connected together in a disorderly way	**touching** at a single point but not intersecting; a sudden digression or change of topic within a conversation; no longer **touching** on the subject
adjacent; **touching**; sharing an edge or boundary	to twist together; making it complicated to free two things from **touching**

More Greek and Latin Roots • 4–8 © 2007 Creative Teaching Press

Read-Around Review: tact, tang, tag, tig

I have the first card.

Who has the roots that mean **touch**?

I have the word **contagious**.

Who has the word that describes what long hair is like first thing in the morning?

I have the roots **tact**, **tang**, **tag**, and **tig**.

Who has the word that means to twist together so that it's complicated to free two things from **touching**?

I have the word **tangled**.

Who has the word that describes an activity that involves actions with the hands or fingers?

I have the word **entangle**.

Who has the word that describes a food or sauce that has a sharp taste or flavor?

I have the word **tactile**.

Who has the word that names what it is called when a person is talking and then strays onto another subject?

I have the word **tangy**.

Who has the word that means that something is whole or complete?

I have the word **tangent**.

Who has the word that describes what you have with someone when you **touch** them?

I have the word **intact**.

Who has the word that means that something is able to be **touched** because it physically exists?

I have the word **contact**.

Who has the word that describes two things that are next to each other, such as two states or office buildings?

I have the word **tangible**.

Who has the word that describes what a person is if he or she can spread germs that make another person ill?

I have the word **contiguous**.

Who has the first card?

Name _____   Date _____

Vocabulary Quiz: tact, tang, tag, tig

Shade in the bubble for the correct word.

1 It's good when a person can keep in *this* with friends that have moved away.
Ⓐ **contact**   Ⓑ **tangible**   Ⓒ **entangle**   Ⓓ **tactile**

2 Some people have a preference for this type of learning because they learn best by manipulating objects.
Ⓐ **tangy**   Ⓑ **tactile**   Ⓒ **tangent**   Ⓓ **contiguous**

3 "Just remember to stay on the topic and avoid *this* when you present your report to the class."
Ⓐ **tangents**   Ⓑ **tangles**   Ⓒ **contagious**   Ⓓ **contact**

4 In elementary schools, desks are pushed together so that students can share the tabletop. "What word below describes their desks?"
Ⓐ **intact**   Ⓑ **tangled**   Ⓒ **tangible**   Ⓓ **contiguous**

5 The sauces in many types of Asian cuisine are famous for this taste.
Ⓐ **tangy**   Ⓑ **tactile**   Ⓒ **tangled**   Ⓓ **contiguous**

6 Although the robot fell from the table, all of its parts were still in place. "What is another word for *in place*?"
Ⓐ **intact**   Ⓑ **contact**   Ⓒ **contagious**   Ⓓ **contiguous**

7 Many magicians perform a popular act in which rings that are entwined, or *this*, suddenly separate.
Ⓐ **contact**   Ⓑ **intact**   Ⓒ **tangible**   Ⓓ **tangled**

8 Chicken pox is *this* type of disease because it is easy to catch it from another person.
Ⓐ **contiguous**   Ⓑ **contagious**   Ⓒ **tactile**   Ⓓ **entangled**

9 One popular game involves people who spin a color, and then put a hand or a foot on the same color of the mat. Soon their bodies get twisted together! "What is another word for *twisted together*?"
Ⓐ **contiguous**   Ⓑ **intact**   Ⓒ **tangy**   Ⓓ **entangled**

10 Which word below could be used to describe a table, chair, or a pencil?
Ⓐ **entangled**   Ⓑ **tangent**   Ⓒ **tangy**   Ⓓ **tangible**

Write the correct word on the line so that the sentence makes sense and sounds grammatically correct.

11 The speaker went off on a _____, talking about her pets instead of explaining how thunderstorms form.

12 All of the states in the United States except for two are _____.

13 A basketball, backpack, and a book are all _____ objects.

14 Max's illness was _____, so he avoided being around other people until he was better.

15 Susie learns best with hands-on activities. She is a _____ learner.

86

Review Test: aud, son, phon, tact, tang, tag, tig

Write the correct word from the word bank to complete each sentence.

Word Bank
assonance
audible
audio
auditorium
cacophony
contact
contagious
contiguous
entangle
intact
phonograph
resonate
sonar
sonnet
tactile
tangent
tangible
tangled
tangy
unison

1. For the upcoming talent show, the three friends are planning to sing the theme song from their favorite show in _____.

2. When she decided to become a nun, Sister Theresa gave up all of her _____ worldly possessions to devote her life to her studies.

3. The writing professor will lower the grade of any piece of writing that goes off on a _____ rather than staying on topic.

4. The little girl got her lollipop _____ in her hair, so she ended up with an unexpected haircut.

5. Sam's whispers were so quiet that they were barely _____ to her friend who was trying to listen.

6. It may sound simple, but writing a quality 14-line _____ is far more difficult than one would imagine.

7. She lost _____ with her best friend when she moved from Mexico to Brazil.

8. Zach felt terrible when he accidentally knocked over the vase on the table. Fortunately, it was still _____.

9. Linda enjoys letting the sounds of the orchestra instruments _____ as she listens to the performance.

10. Many condos or townhomes are considered to be _____, because they share a common wall.

11. My ears are still throbbing! What a _____ it was in there!

12. If you turn off the _____ feature, you can read the subtitles and still understand what is happening in the movie.

13. What did you add to this salad? It tastes so _____ and delicious.

14. They say that a smile is _____, so if you smile, someone else might too!

15. The choir was rehearsing for its final performance in the school's _____.

Word List: clud, clus, claus = to close

Vocabulary	Definitions
clause (n)	a group of words containing a subject and a predicate, and forming part of a compound or complex sentence
claustrophobia (n)	an abnormal fear of narrow or **closed** spaces
cluster (n)	a group of the same or similar elements **close** together
conclude (v)	to end; **to close** an event, book, or movie; to decide
enclose (v)	**to close** in; to surround on all sides
exclude (v)	to keep out; to prevent from entering; to keep **closed** off
exclusive (adj)	private; **closed** to those not permitted; single or sole
preclude (v)	**to close** off or prevent from a given activity
reclusive (adj)	seeking to be **closed** off from others; preferring to be isolated and alone
secluded (adj)	kept apart from others; **closed** off; private

KEEP OUT!

More Greek and Latin Roots • 4–8 © 2007 Creative Teaching Press

Vocabulary Sort: clud, clus, claus

exclude	reclusive	enclose	clause	exclusive
secluded	conclude	cluster	preclude	claustrophobia

to end; **to close** an event, book, or movie; to decide	**to close** off or prevent from a given activity
kept apart from others; **closed** off; private	a group of the same or similar elements **close** together
to keep out; to prevent from entering; to keep **closed** off	private; **closed** to those not permitted; single or sole
an abnormal fear of narrow or **closed** spaces	seeking to be **closed** off from others; preferring to be isolated and alone
to close in; to surround on all sides	a group of words containing a subject and a predicate, and forming part of a compound or complex sentence

More Greek and Latin Roots • 4–8 © 2007 Creative Teaching Press

Read-Around Review: clud, clus, claus

I have the first card. Who has the roots that mean **to close**?	I have the word **enclose**. Who has the word that describes a private place, such as an island or home, that is far from other people?
I have the roots **clud**, **clus**, **claus**. Who has the word that describes when something is kept from happening?	I have the word **secluded**. Who has the word that identifies what you do when you finish a story or book?
I have the word **preclude**. Who has the word that identifies an abnormal fear of **closed** spaces, such as elevators?	I have the word **conclude**. Who has the word that identifies a group of similar objects sharing a small space?
I have the word **claustrophobia**. Who has the word that describes a club or location that only allows certain favored people to enter?	I have the word **cluster**. Who has the word that identifies the part of a compound or complex sentence that contains a subject and predicate?
I have the word **exclusive**. Who has the word that describes a person who lives by himself and purposely avoids any contact with people?	I have the word **clause**. Who has the word that means to purposely leave something out?
I have the word **reclusive**. Who has the word that describes what you do when you place a cage around an animal for protection?	I have the word **exclude**. Who has the first card?

More Greek and Latin Roots • 4–8 © 2007 Creative Teaching Press

Name _____   Date _____

Vocabulary Quiz: clud, clus, claus

Shade in the bubble for the correct word.

1 The Lee family purchased tickets to this type of resort, which is usually only available to celebrities.
   Ⓐ **reclusive**   Ⓑ **exclusive**   Ⓒ **clustered**   Ⓓ **enclosed**

2 Because Molly didn't turn her homework in on time her mother will do *this* by preventing her from attending the Fall Ball.
   Ⓐ **preclude**   Ⓑ **secluded**   Ⓒ **exclusive**   Ⓓ **claustrophobic**

3 The grapes on the vine were hanging close together in *this* waiting to be picked at harvest time.
   Ⓐ **exclude**   Ⓑ **secluded**   Ⓒ **clause**   Ⓓ **cluster**

4 Chain link fences installed around playgrounds do *this* to the area to keep the children safe.
   Ⓐ **enclose**   Ⓑ **reclusive**   Ⓒ **secluded**   Ⓓ **conclude**

5 Although the tour of the bat caves sounded exciting, Mike opted out because of his intense fear of small spaces. "What word below describes his fear?"
   Ⓐ **clusters**   Ⓑ **exclusions**   Ⓒ **enclosures**   Ⓓ **claustrophobia**

6 Based on the evidence, the judge agreed that the defendant was guilty as charged. "What did the judge do?"
   Ⓐ **include**   Ⓑ **seclude**   Ⓒ **conclude**   Ⓓ **exclude**

7 In most businesses, it is illegal to do this to people based on race or gender.
   Ⓐ **exclude**   Ⓑ **reclusive**   Ⓒ **include**   Ⓓ **cluster**

8 A person who prefers to be alone rather than interact with others may be described as *this*.
   Ⓐ **claustrophobic**   Ⓑ **clustered**   Ⓒ **exclusive**   Ⓓ **reclusive**

9 What word below describes a private beach with no one around for miles?
   Ⓐ **clustered**   Ⓑ **secluded**   Ⓒ **claustrophobic**   Ⓓ **enclosed**

10 There are many different forms of this part of a sentence, but they all have a subject and predicate.
   Ⓐ **cluster**   Ⓑ **recluse**   Ⓒ **conclusion**   Ⓓ **clause**

Write the correct word on the line so that the sentence makes sense and sounds grammatically correct.

11 A person who obtains a copyright has _____ permission to reproduce the written material.

12 Some people are _____ and prefer to live alone and have no contact with others.

13 The cabin was hard to find because it was _____ in the mountains.

14 "After listening to both sides of the argument, I must _____ that you are both incorrect on many issues."

15 The flower bulbs were planted in a _____ so that they would bloom in groups.

Word List: spond, spons, spous = promise, answer for, pledge

Vocabulary	Definitions
correspond (v)	to be similar; coincides; goes with; to **answer** through writing
despondent (adj)	without hope or **promise**; forlorn; hopeless
espouse (v)	to **pledge** one's loyalty to; to support
irresponsible (adj)	not reliable; untrustworthy; not **answering for** one's actions
respond (v)	to **answer**; to make a reply
responsible (adj)	reliable; worthy of trust; to **answer for** one's actions
responsive (adj)	**answering**; reacting
sponsor (v)	to assume responsibility for someone else; to **promise** to pay for someone's expenses
spontaneous (adj)	unplanned; happening without an external cause; no **promise** of a plan
spouse (n)	a marriage partner; a person who **pledged** marriage

More Greek and Latin Roots • 4–8 © 2007 Creative Teaching Press

Vocabulary Sort: spond, spons, spous

sponsor	espouse	despondent	correspond	spouse
responsive	respond	responsible	irresponsible	spontaneous

to **answer**; to make a reply	to **pledge** one's loyalty to; to support
to be similar; coincides; goes with; to **answer** through writing	a marriage partner; a person who **pledged** marriage
answering; reacting	to assume responsibility for someone else; to **promise** to pay for someone's expenses
not reliable; untrustworthy; not **answering for** one's actions	without hope or **promise**; forlorn; hopeless
unplanned; happening without an external cause; no **promise** of a plan	reliable; worthy of trust; **answering for** one's actions

Read-Around Review: spond, spons, spous

I have the first card.

Who has the roots that mean to **promise**, **answer for**, and **pledge**?

I have the roots **spond**, **spons**, and **spous**.

Who has the word that means to **promise** to pay for the expenses of someone else?

I have the word **sponsor**.

Who has the word that describes a person who is able to communicate in some way after being in a serious accident?

I have the word **responsive**.

Who has the word that describes an action that was unplanned, such as a cheer at a game?

I have the word **spontaneous**.

Who has the word that describes a person who makes **promises** but doesn't keep them?

I have the word **irresponsible**.

Who has the word that identifies a marriage partner?

I have the word **spouse**.

Who has the word that describes what you do when you **answer** a question?

I have the word **respond**.

Who has the word that describes a person who feels hopeless?

I have the word **despondent**.

Who has the word that means to send letters, e-mails, or text messages back and forth?

I have the word **correspond**.

Who has the word that describes what you are doing when you declare a loyalty to a person or cause?

I have the word **espouse**.

Who has the word that describes a person who is reliable and trustworthy?

I have the word **responsible**.

Who has the first card?

More Greek and Latin Roots • 4–8 © 2007 Creative Teaching Press

Vocabulary Quiz: spond, spons, spous

Shade in the bubble for the correct word.

1 Pen pals typically write letters back and forth to each other, but e-mailing is becoming more common. "What are pen pals doing?"
    Ⓐ **espousing**   Ⓑ **sponsoring**   Ⓒ **responding**   Ⓓ **corresponding**

2 Which word below describes the type of person you should look for when choosing a pet sitter?
    Ⓐ **responsible**   Ⓑ **spontaneous**   Ⓒ **despondent**   Ⓓ **irresponsible**

3 The medics on an ambulance are trained to help people even when they are unconscious or *this*.
    Ⓐ **irresponsible**   Ⓑ **unresponsive**   Ⓒ **sponsored**   Ⓓ **spontaneous**

4 The married couple promised to care for each other in all cases. "What word below describes their loyalty?"
    Ⓐ **espoused**   Ⓑ **responded**   Ⓒ **sponsored**   Ⓓ **corresponded**

5 Joe was feeling this way because he was disappointed in himself when he lost his job.
    Ⓐ **despondent**   Ⓑ **responsible**   Ⓒ **responsive**   Ⓓ **spontaneous**

6 A person who is not reliable will not make a good leader. "What word below describes this type of person?"
    Ⓐ **sponsor**   Ⓑ **despondent**   Ⓒ **spouse**   Ⓓ **irresponsible**

7 Mr. and Mrs. Schmitz are married. "What word below describes their relationship to one another?"
    Ⓐ **irresponsible**   Ⓑ **spouses**   Ⓒ **sponsors**   Ⓓ **despondent**

8 On his way home from work, Joe saw a jewelry store and decided to stop and buy his mother a bracelet. "What word below describes Joe's actions?"
    Ⓐ **spontaneous**   Ⓑ **sponsor**   Ⓒ **espouse**   Ⓓ **correspondence**

9 Trenton's aunt agreed to pay for his expenses in the upcoming marathon. "What did Trenton's aunt become?"
    Ⓐ **irresponsible**   Ⓑ **spouse**   Ⓒ **spontaneous**   Ⓓ **sponsor**

10 If you see the acronym RSVP on an invitation, you need to let the person know if you will be attending the party. "What does the *R* stand for in English?"
    Ⓐ **responsive**   Ⓑ **resubmit**   Ⓒ **respond**   Ⓓ **responsible**

Write the correct word on the line so that the sentence makes sense and sounds grammatically correct.

11 Are you still _____ with your grandmother via the postal mail or e-mail?

12 A person who is unconscious would not be _____ to noise or movement.

13 The audience _____ began to yell, "BOO!"

14 Take a few moments to think about positive things if you ever begin to feel _____.

15 *Irresponsible* is to *untrustworthy* as _____ is to *trustworthy*.

Name _____   Date _____

Review Test: clud, clus, claus, spond, spons, spous

Write the correct word from the word bank to complete each sentence.

1 Would you like to join me on a trip to see the _____ island resort of Bora Bora, where you won't see any other people for miles?

2 A person who spends more money than he saves might be described as _____.

3 While Art was away running a fishing resort in Alaska, the only way to _____ with him was by mail.

4 A psychologist is trained at helping _____ people find hope and focus on the good things in life.

5 Sam was such a talented runner that his opponents tried to _____ him from the race saying that he was too old.

6 The Martinez family has plans to _____ their back deck so that even on rainy days they can enjoy picnics outside.

7 Anyone who plans on being a babysitter needs to prove that he or she is _____ enough to handle the job.

8 Dane wanted to sell his train set and was waiting for someone to _____ to his ad.

9 Although Winnie was a bit _____, she had no problem walking through the secret underground caverns.

10 "And in _____, I'd like to thank my mother for the many sacrifices she made to ensure that I received a good education."

11 "Our next stop will be outside the gates of the most _____ part of the city, the S.D.S. Country Club."

12 Some big corporations will _____ an athlete to promote their product.

13 Within the school, there was a small _____ of parents who volunteered.

14 Without thinking, she threw her hat into the audience. What a _____ move! Even she wasn't expecting to do that!

15 If your toes twitch while being tickled you are _____ to touch.

clause
claustrophobic
cluster
conclusion
correspond
despondent
enclose
espouse
exclude
exclusive
irresponsible
preclude
reclusive
respond
responsible
responsive
secluded
sponsor
spontaneous
spouse

More Greek and Latin Roots • 4–8 © 2007 Creative Teaching Press

Word List: pot, pos, val = power, to be strong

Vocabulary	Definitions
despot (n)	a ruler with absolute **power**; a tyrant
devalue (v)	to lessen in value or **strength**
impotent (adj)	lacking in **strength**, vigor, or **power**; helpless
nepotism (n)	using **power** in a business to grant favors to a relative
omnipotent (adj)	all **powerful**; having unlimited **power** or authority
possess (v)	to have; to take possession; having the **power**
potent (adj)	possessing inner **strength**; **powerful**; capable of having a **strong** influence
potential (n)	possessing the ability to grow or develop
potion (n)	a **powerful** liquid or mixture that is thought to be medicinal, poisonous, or magical
valor (n)	courage; boldness; bravery; **to be strong** in mind or spirit

More Greek and Latin Roots • 4-8 © 2007 Creative Teaching Press

Vocabulary Sort: pot, pos, val

omnipotent	nepotism	devalue	valor	potion
potent	despot	impotent	possess	potential

using **power** in a business to grant favors to a relative	courage; boldness; bravery; **to be strong**
to have; to take possession; having the **power**	a ruler with absolute **power**; a tyrant
possessing the ability to grow or develop	all **powerful**; having unlimited **power** or authority
lacking in **strength**, vigor, or **power**; helpless	a **powerful** liquid or mixture that is thought to be medicinal, poisonous, or magical
possessing inner **strength**; **powerful**; capable of having a **strong** influence	to lessen in value or **strength**

More Greek and Latin Roots • 4–8 © 2007 Creative Teaching Press

Read-Around Review: pot, pos, val

I have the first card. Who has the roots that mean **power** or **to be strong**?	I have the word **nepotism**. Who has the word that describes a character trait that many heroes are said to possess?
I have the roots **pot**, **pos**, and **val**. Who has the word that means to have the control or **power** over something?	I have the word **valor**. Who has the word that means to lessen the **strength** or worthiness of something, such as when a person is ridiculed?
I have the word **possess**. Who has the word that describes a situation in which one might feel helpless and without any control?	I have the word **devalue**. Who has the word that describes what a person has if he or she is able to grow **stronger** in an area or activity?
I have the word **impotent**. Who has the word that identifies a liquid that is said to have special **powers** of healing or magic?	I have the word **potential**. Who has the word that identifies someone who is viewed negatively because they use their power in a cruel way?
I have the word **potion**. Who has the word that describes a person who has complete **power** in a situation?	I have the word **despot**. Who has the word that describes **strength** that can be used as an influence?
I have the word **omnipotent**. Who has the word that describes what people are doing if they run a company and hire their children as employees.	I have the word **potent**. Who has the first card?

More Greek and Latin Roots • 4–8 © 2007 Creative Teaching Press

Name _____   Date _____

Vocabulary Quiz: pot, pos, val

Shade in the bubble for the correct word.

1 "That strong comment will certainly convince people to take action." "What word describes the comment?"
  Ⓐ potent   Ⓑ valor   Ⓒ nepotism   Ⓓ devalue

2 In many fairy tales, the villain offers this substance to lure a character.
  Ⓐ potential   Ⓑ impotent   Ⓒ potion   Ⓓ despot

3 Sergeant Wise was awarded a medal of honor for his bravery. "What word below is a synonym for bravery?"
  Ⓐ omnipotent   Ⓑ valor   Ⓒ impotent   Ⓓ nepotism

4 Sean said, "I didn't mean to hurt your feelings. I should have kept my criticism to myself." "How did Sean's original comments make the other person feel?"
  Ⓐ despot   Ⓑ impotent   Ⓒ potential   Ⓓ devalued

5 Because Steve displayed this characteristic, his instructors could tell he would become a talented doctor.
  Ⓐ potential   Ⓑ potion   Ⓒ devalue   Ⓓ nepotism

6 In the aftermath of the devastating hurricanes, the relief workers felt helpless and overwhelmed. "What word below describes how they were feeling?"
  Ⓐ impotent   Ⓑ possess   Ⓒ potential   Ⓓ omnipotent

7 Mrs. Lang's daughter was not allowed to work at the same site as her mother for fear they would be accused of *this*.
  Ⓐ despot   Ⓑ valor   Ⓒ omnipotent   Ⓓ nepotism

8 Some rulers in history were known as tyrants. "What is another word for *tyrants*?"
  Ⓐ devalue   Ⓑ nepotism   Ⓒ despots   Ⓓ possess

9 Dr. Petersen has a gift for unique approaches to mathematical calculations. "What is another word for *has*?"
  Ⓐ possesses   Ⓑ omnipotent   Ⓒ valor   Ⓓ despot

10 Which word below describes someone viewed as having complete power or authority?
  Ⓐ omnipotent   Ⓑ potential   Ⓒ nepotism   Ⓓ despotism

Write the correct word on the line so that the sentence makes sense and sounds grammatically correct.

11 Dr. Abdul specializes in herbal remedies, but his medicines look more like _____ in those glass vials.

12 He knew that he had the _____ to get better grades if only he would study more often.

13 Tracy felt _____ when Cal said he didn't think her artwork was even worthy of the garage.

14 *Fear* is to *cowardice* as *bravery* is to _____.

15 *Potent* is to *strength and power* as _____ is to *helpless and powerless*.

More Greek and Latin Roots • 4–8 © 2007 Creative Teaching Press

Word List: cit, civ, poli, polis, polit = citizen, city, state*

Vocabulary	Definitions
citadel (n)	a fortress in a commanding position in or near a **city**; a fortified place
citation (n)	a ticket; a violation of a minor law within a **city** or **state**
civil (adj)	peaceable behavior; public order; following the laws of a **city** or **state**
civilization (n)	a group of people who live together; the way of life of a people having reached a civilized state
metropolis (n)	a major **city**; a **city** or urban area regarded as the center of a specific activity
necropolis (n)	a large and elaborate cemetery belonging to an ancient **city;** a historic or prehistoric burial ground
police (v)	to control, regulate, or keep order (especially as an official duty of a **city**)
policy (n)	a plan or course of action of a **city**, **state**, or other organization
politician (n)	one who holds a political office in a **city** or **state**
politics (n)	the activities, methods, tactics, or affairs associated with the government of a **city** or **state**

* In this instance, the word "state" means any politically organized group of people occupying and controlling a definite territory, such as a country

Vocabulary Sort: cit, civ, poli, polis, polit

metropolis	civil	police	citadel	civilization
policy	necropolis	politician	politics	citation

one who holds a political office in a **city** or **state**	a group of people who live together; the way of life of a people having reached a civilized state
a plan or course of action of a **city**, **state**, or other organization	a ticket; a violation of a minor law within a **city** or **state**
a major **city**; a **city** or urban area regarded as the center of a specific activity	a large and elaborate cemetery belonging to an ancient **city**; a historic or prehistoric burial ground
to control, regulate, or keep order (especially as an official duty of a **city**)	the activities, methods, tactics, or affairs associated with the government of a **city** or **state**
a fortress in a commanding position in or near a **city**; a fortified place	peaceable behavior; public order; following the laws of a **city** or **state**

More Greek and Latin Roots • 4–8 © 2007 Creative Teaching Press

Read-Around Review: cit, civ, poli, polis, polit

I have the first card.

Who has the roots that mean **citizen**, **city**, or **state**?

I have the word **policy**.

Who has the word that identifies what someone will receive if they break a minor law, such as a traffic violation for speeding?

I have the roots **cit**, **civ**, **poli**, **polis**, and **polit**.

Who has the word that identifies a group of people, such as the ancient Greeks, who live together in a complex society?

I have the word **citation**.

Who has the word that means a person who holds a political office, such as a mayor or governor?

I have the word **civilization**.

Who has the word that names the action of watching over others to be sure they follow the rules?

I have the word **politician**.

Who has the word that identifies a major **city** that will often have taller buildings and more businesses than surrounding cities?

I have the word **police**.

Who has the word that identifies an ancient burial ground?

I have the word **metropolis**.

Who has the word that identifies the activities, methods, or dealings within a governmental office or workplace?

I have the word **necropolis**.

Who has the word that describes the ability to live peaceably with others?

I have the word **politics**.

Who has the word that identifies a fortress or fortified structure?

I have the word **civil**.

Who has the word that identifies a plan of a **city**, organization, or business that lists what to do in different situations?

I have the word **citadel**.

Who has the first card?

More Greek and Latin Roots • 4–8 © 2007 Creative Teaching Press

Name _____   Date _____

Vocabulary Quiz: cit, civ, poli, polis, polit

Shade in the bubble for the correct word.

1 Which word below describes a person elected by the people to represent them in decisions that effect the policies of a government?
Ⓐ **metropolis**　　Ⓑ **politician**　　Ⓒ **citation**　　Ⓓ **policy**

2 In middle school, most students enjoy learning about the ancient societies of Rome, Greece, and Sparta, which we also call *these*.
Ⓐ **metropolis**　　Ⓑ **civilizations**　　Ⓒ **citadels**　　Ⓓ **policies**

3 The archaeologists were amazed at their discovery of skulls while searching for ruins of the ancient civilization. "They most likely found what place?"
Ⓐ **necropolis**　　Ⓑ **metropolis**　　Ⓒ **citadels**　　Ⓓ **politician**

4 For safety reasons, most parents will do this with their children's use of cell phones and the Internet.
Ⓐ **police**　　Ⓑ **civil**　　Ⓒ **citations**　　Ⓓ **metropolis**

5 Trey received a traffic ticket or *this* because he did not come to a complete stop at the stop sign.
Ⓐ **citadel**　　Ⓑ **civil**　　Ⓒ **metropolis**　　Ⓓ **citation**

6 What word below describes a large and busy city with skyscrapers and busy streets?
Ⓐ **metropolis**　　Ⓑ **civilization**　　Ⓒ **citadel**　　Ⓓ **necropolis**

7 The babysitter wanted the twins to cooperate and be nice to each other, or act *this* way.
Ⓐ **civil**　　Ⓑ **necropolis**　　Ⓒ **citation**　　Ⓓ **politics**

8 The famous mountaintop fortress, Machu Picchu, is in Peru. "What is another word for this fortress?"
Ⓐ **civilization**　　Ⓑ **citadel**　　Ⓒ **policy**　　Ⓓ **citation**

9 Every school has rules that students need to follow. "What is another name for these rules?"
Ⓐ **civil**　　Ⓑ **policies**　　Ⓒ **citations**　　Ⓓ **politics**

10 People who are interested in *this* are concerned with guiding or influencing governmental policies.
Ⓐ **politics**　　Ⓑ **civil**　　Ⓒ **citadels**　　Ⓓ **police**

Write the correct word on the line so that the sentence makes sense and sounds grammatically correct.

11 Linda was disappointed when she received her first _____ after 20 years of safe driving.

12 It's the official _____ of most stores to allow a person to return merchandise.

13 Many teenagers misunderstand why their parents and loved ones _____ their activities.

14 The _____ was built to protect the king and his castle.

15 *Tiny little village* is to _____ as *car* is to *semi-truck*.

104

More Greek and Latin Roots • 4–8 © 2007 Creative Teaching Press

Name _____ Date _____

Review Test: pot, pos, val, cit, civ, poli, polis, polit

Write the correct word from the word bank to complete each sentence.

1 Afraid that he might be accused of _____, the president of the corporation chose not to hire his daughter.

2 When it came to decision making within the household, Donald felt _____ and helpless.

3 Darcy was upset with the "No Pets Allowed" _____ posted in the windows of most stores.

4 If you visit Vietnam, you can see the famous Kinh Thien Palace situated in the heart of the Forbidden _____, which was the headquarters during the war.

5 Growing up in Kansas, Dorothy had never before seen a _____ full of skyscrapers, taxicabs, and corporations.

6 Everyone is born with the _____ to achieve great things in life.

7 It was such a _____ batch of wasabi that one tiny taste on sushi would make a person's nose burn and eyes water.

8 Even the leader of a modern, civilized nation cannot be _____, because there are usually others who share control of major decisions.

9 Kristin _____ an outstanding ability to sing, so she was invited to appear on a television talent show.

10 At most schools, there are teachers, students, and a principal who help _____ the area to make sure everyone is making good choices.

11 Students who demonstrate mutual respect act _____ toward one another.

12 Believe it or not, a dog will occasionally receive a Medal of _____ for rescuing a child in a life-threatening situation.

13 "I can't wait to learn about the ancient _____ of China, Egypt, and India."

14 In some schools, students who serve as hall monitors may issue _____ to people who run in the hallway.

15 When the money of a country is _____, it buys less and can negatively effect businesses and other countries.

Word Bank

citadel
citations
civilizations
civilly
despot
devalued
impotent
metropolis
necropolis
nepotism
omnipotent
police
policy
politician
politics
possessed
potent
potential
potion
valor

More Greek and Latin Roots • 4–8 © 2007 Creative Teaching Press

Word List: fac, fic, fect, fict = make, do

Vocabulary	Definitions
affect (v)	to have an influence on or **make** a change in
benefactor (n)	a person who gives aid (especially financial aid); a person who **does** helpful things for another person; a person who donates money
deface (v)	to disfigure; to ruin the surface; to destroy by **doing** something to the object
defect (v)	something people **do** when they abandon a position or association, often to join the opposing group
effect (n)	the result; something brought about by a cause or by **doing**
facilitate (v)	to **make** easier
factor (n)	something that actively contributes to an accomplishment, result, or process; something that helps **make** something else happen
factory (n)	a building or group of buildings in which a product is **made**; a plant
infect (v)	to contaminate; to **make** ill; to corrupt
manufacture (v)	to **make**, create, or produce

More Greek and Latin Roots • 4–8 © 2007 Creative Teaching Press

Vocabulary Sort: fac, fic, fect, fict

factor	infect	affect	effect	defect
deface	benefactor	facilitate	factory	manufacture

something people **do** when they abandon a position or association, often to join the opposing group	to **make** easier
a building or group of buildings in which a product is **made**; a plant	a person who gives aid (especially financial aid); a person who **does** helpful things for another person; a person who donates money
to have an influence on or **make** a change in	to contaminate; to **make** ill; to corrupt
to **make**, create, or produce	something that actively contributes to an accomplishment, result, or process; something that helps **make** something else happen
to disfigure; to ruin the surface; to destroy by **doing** something to the object	the result; something brought about by a cause or by **doing**

More Greek and Latin Roots • 4–8 © 2007 Creative Teaching Press

Read-Around Review: fac, fic, fect, fict

I have the first card.

Who has the roots that mean to **make** or **do**?

I have the word **facilitate**.

Who has the word that names what people **do** when they switch sides?

I have the roots **fac**, **fic**, **fect**, **fict**.

Who has the word that identifies a building in which consumer goods, such as cereals, jeans, or cars, are **made**?

I have the word **defect**.

Who has the word that identifies something that is directly responsible for something that occurs?

I have the word **factory**.

Who has the word that names what happens as a result of falling, such as breaking a leg?

I have the word **factor**.

Who has the word that names what people **do** when they ruin something, such as property?

I have the word **effect**.

Who has the word that identifies a person who donates money?

I have the word **deface**.

Who has the word that describes what happens when factories create items for sale in stores around the world?

I have the word **benefactor**.

Who has the word that identifies what people **do** when they spread germs and others get sick as a result?

I have the word **manufacture**.

Who has the word that names what happens when something influences something else?

I have the word **infect**.

Who has the word that names what you do when you **make** something easier and often faster?

I have the word **affect**.

Who has the first card?

More Greek and Latin Roots • 4–8 © 2007 Creative Teaching Press

Vocabulary Quiz: fac, fic, fect, fict

Shade in the bubble for the correct word.

1 A tutor can do *this* with a student's learning to help make it easier.
    Ⓐ **benefactor**   Ⓑ **facilitate**   Ⓒ **deface**   Ⓓ **manufacture**

2 Two things that played a key role in her success were her education and the support of her parents. "What is another word for these two things?"
    Ⓐ **factors**   Ⓑ **defects**   Ⓒ **affects**   Ⓓ **effects**

3 A nonprofit group decided to make and sell baskets to help individuals with physical and mental challenges. "What is another word for *make*?"
    Ⓐ **manufacture**   Ⓑ **deface**   Ⓒ **defect**   Ⓓ **benefactors**

4 Many people believe that their allergies are impacted or *this* by the weather conditions.
    Ⓐ **infected**   Ⓑ **affected**   Ⓒ **effected**   Ⓓ **defected**

5 A group of generous people funded an organization to help children better prepare for our technological society. "What word below describes these generous people?"
    Ⓐ **manufacturers**   Ⓑ **facilitators**   Ⓒ **defectors**   Ⓓ **benefactors**

6 Mary was sick, so she stayed home to avoid doing *this* to others.
    Ⓐ **infecting**   Ⓑ **defecting**   Ⓒ **effecting**   Ⓓ **factoring**

7 Which word describes the result of Sonny breaking his leg after hitting a tree while skiing down a hill?
    Ⓐ **effect**   Ⓑ **affect**   Ⓒ **defect**   Ⓓ **benefactor**

8 Each section of this type of building was dedicated to a different stage of the construction of handbags.
    Ⓐ **manufacture**   Ⓑ **defect**   Ⓒ **facilitate**   Ⓓ **factory**

9 When a student writes on a desk, he or she is doing this to public property.
    Ⓐ **affecting**   Ⓑ **defacing**   Ⓒ **defecting**   Ⓓ **infecting**

10 As a result of the civil unrest in his native country, Salvador did *this* and moved to another country.
    Ⓐ **defected**   Ⓑ **infected**   Ⓒ **affected**   Ⓓ **infected**

Write the correct word on the line so that the sentence makes sense and sounds grammatically correct.

11 Steve didn't know if his sad poem would _____ the audience at the Annual Poetry Reading.

12 In order to _____ the process of getting his taxes done, Frank's tax preparer sent forms and a questionnaire to be completed before their appointment.

13 Getting enough sleep is one _____ that helps us grow up healthy.

14 *Nurse* is to *patient* as _____ is to *charity* or *needy cause*.

15 *Question* is to *answer* as *cause* is to _____.

Word List: mim, sembl, simil, simul = copy, imitate, to make like, together

Vocabulary	Definitions
assemble (v)	to put or bring **together**
assimilate (v)	**to make alike**; to mentally absorb; to incorporate
ensemble (n)	a coordinated outfit, group, or set; a group of parts that go **together**
facsimile (n)	a fax; an exact **copy**; a duplicate
mimic (v)	to **copy** or **imitate** closely
resemble (v)	to exhibit a **likeness** to something; to look **like** something else
semblance (adj)	an outward or token appearance; a **copy**; a representation
simile (n)	a figure of speech in which two unlike things are compared as if they are **alike**
simulation (n)	an **imitation** of an event; a reproduction of an event that is similar to the actual event
simultaneous (adj)	happening, existing, or done at the same time; done **together**

More Greek and Latin Roots • 4–8 © 2007 Creative Teaching Press

Vocabulary Sort: mim, sembl, simil, simul

assimilate	simile	ensemble	simulation	simultaneous
assemble	facsimile	mimic	resemble	semblance

an outward or token appearance; a **copy**; a representation	happening, existing, or done at the same time; done **together**
to **copy** or **imitate** closely	to exhibit a **likeness** to something; to look **like** something else
to put or bring **together**	**to make alike**; to mentally absorb; to incorporate
a figure of speech in which two unlike things are compared as if they are **alike**	an **imitation** of an event; a reproduction of an event that is similar to the actual event
a coordinated outfit, group, or set; a group of parts that go **together**	a fax; an exact **copy**; a duplicate

More Greek and Latin Roots • 4–8 © 2007 Creative Teaching Press

Read-Around Review: mim, sembl, simil, simul

I have the first card.

Who has the roots that mean **copy**, **imitate**, **to make like**, or **together**?

I have the word **simile**.

Who has the word that names what a person is doing when he or she is **copying** every single move you make?

I have the roots **mim**, **sembl**, **simil**, and **simul**.

Who has the word that describes things that happen at the same time?

I have the word **mimic**.

Who has the word that describes when one thing only appears to be similar to something else?

I have the word **simultaneous**.

Who has the word that names what something does when it looks just **like** something else?

I have the word **semblance**.

Who has the word that names taking new information and connecting it to prior information?

I have the word **resemble**.

Who has the word that names something you can participate in that is **like** the real event, but is only a replication?

I have the word **assimilate**.

Who has the word that names a group of people, parts, or pieces that fit **together**?

I have the word **simulation**.

Who has the word that names a duplicate of something, such as paperwork that is often sent over a machine?

I have the word **ensemble**.

Who has the word that means to put or bring things **together**, such as people coming together for a meeting?

I have the word **facsimile**.

Who has the word that names the following: *a smile as sweet as sugar*?

I have the word **assemble**.

Who has the first card?

More Greek and Latin Roots • 4–8 © 2007 Creative Teaching Press

Name _____ Date _____

Vocabulary Quiz: mim, sembl, simil, simul

Shade in the bubble for the correct word.

1 Every Friday, the students do *this* in the quad to listen to school announcements.
Ⓐ **resemble**   Ⓑ **ensemble**   Ⓒ **assemble**   Ⓓ **semblance**

2 It's so annoying when someone repeats everything you say. "What is another word for *repeats*?"
Ⓐ **resembles**   Ⓑ **mimics**   Ⓒ **simulates**   Ⓓ **assimilates**

3 "You look like someone I knew when I was in college." "What is another word for *look like*?"
Ⓐ **resemble**   Ⓑ **assimilate**   Ⓒ **mimic**   Ⓓ **simulation**

4 Leroy won the race because he ran as fast as a cheetah! "What is this sentence an example of?"
Ⓐ **simile**   Ⓑ **simulation**   Ⓒ **facsimile**   Ⓓ **simultaneous**

5 On the field trip to the Space Center, the students had a chance to wear the space suits and act out the roles of a team guiding a space shuttle back to Earth. "What word below describes this activity?"
Ⓐ **semblance**   Ⓑ **simile**   Ⓒ **assemble**   Ⓓ **simulation**

6 "Please send me a copy or *this* of your application so that I can add it to your file."
Ⓐ **mimic**   Ⓑ **assimilate**   Ⓒ **facsimile**   Ⓓ **resemble**

7 What word below describes two things that happen at the same time?
Ⓐ **simultaneous**   Ⓑ **simile**   Ⓒ **assemble**   Ⓓ **mimic**

8 Each member of the dance group had a key role, so they were unable to perform unless all members were present. "What is another word for their group?"
Ⓐ **ensemble**   Ⓑ **simultaneous**   Ⓒ **resemble**   Ⓓ **semblance**

9 What are you trying to do when making sense out of information someone is telling you?
Ⓐ **resemble**   Ⓑ **simile**   Ⓒ **facsimile**   Ⓓ **assimilate**

10 There was great similarity between the two pieces of writing. "What is another word for *similarity*?"
Ⓐ **semblance**   Ⓑ **simultaneous**   Ⓒ **mimickry**   Ⓓ **simulation**

Write the correct word on the line so that the sentence makes sense and sounds grammatically correct.

11 Your shoes, purse, and earrings create the perfect _____!

12 When moving to another country, a person must learn to _____ into the culture.

13 Flight school requires many hours of airplane flight _____ before ever actually flying a plane.

14 *Disassemble* is to _____ as *disagree* is to *agree*.

15 *A sea of troubles* is to *metaphor* as *as rich as the day is long* is to _____.

Review Test: fac, fic, fect, fict, mim, sembl, simil, simul

Write the correct word from the word bank to complete each sentence.

1. In order to _____ his upcoming move from America to Japan, Felix took two Japanese classes to better understand the culture.

2. Has anyone ever told you that you _____ the actor who starred in all those movies last year?

3. A parrot can learn to _____ both the words and the intonation of its owner.

4. His grades and his community service are two _____ that will impact his chances of getting into the college or university of his choice.

5. Two _____ provided the community theater with additional funding, which allowed for the construction to be completed.

6. People who _____ public property are often punished by the law enforcement agencies.

7. There were devastating _____ suffered by the people when the tsunami suddenly hit many areas of Thailand in 2004.

8. In history class, they were reenacting the War of 1812. What an incredible _____!

9. Luigi's parents owned a _____ that _____ pasta noodles that were sold in fine restaurants around the world.

10. The movie was so hysterical that Kate was laughing and crying _____.

11. She did not want to _____ her classmates, so she sneezed into her arm rather than her hand.

12. The highest-rated television show consists of an _____ cast of five characters. The show wouldn't be the same if any one of the five left.

13. The tour guide asked everyone to _____ at 3:00 in the Tea Room for afternoon tea in the traditional British style.

14. Your decisions today will _____ your life tomorrow.

15. When giving an apology, it's important to show some _____ of remorse.

Word Bank

affect
assemble
assimilate
benefactors
deface
defect
effects
ensemble
facilitate
facsimile
factors
factory
infect
manufactured
mimic
resemble
semblance
simile
simulation
simultaneously

More Greek and Latin Roots • 4–8 © 2007 Creative Teaching Press

Word List: leg, lect = law, choose, gather, select, read

Vocabulary	Definitions
allege (v)	to state; to report or maintain an opinion without or before proof
allegory (n)	a symbolic representation; a story, picture, or play employing representation
delegate (v)	to authorize or send as one's **chosen** representative; to entrust to another
election (n)	the process of voting to **choose** a winner
electorate (n)	a group of qualified voters
legalize (v)	to make **lawful**; to authorize
legible (adj)	possible to decipher; capable of being **read**
legislation (n)	the making or giving of **laws**; an enacted **law**
legitimate (adj)	**lawful**; authentic; genuine
privilege (n)	a special advantage, permission, right, or benefit

More Greek and Latin Roots • 4–8 © 2007 Creative Teaching Press

Vocabulary Sort: leg, lect

legible	legitimate	allegory	allege	privilege
legalize	legislation	delegate	election	electorate

to authorize or send as one's **chosen** representative; to entrust to another	a symbolic representation; a story, picture, or play employing representation
lawful; authentic; genuine	a special advantage, permission, right, or benefit
to state; to report or maintain an opinion without or before proof	to make **lawful**; to authorize
the process of voting to **choose** a winner	a group of qualified voters
the making or giving of **laws**; an enacted **law**	possible to decipher; capable of being **read**

More Greek and Latin Roots • 4–8 © 2007 Creative Teaching Press

Read-Around Review: leg, lect

I have the first card. Who has the roots that mean **law**, **choose**, **gather**, **select**, or **read**?	I have the word **election**. Who has the word that describes something that is neat enough to **read**?
I have the roots **leg** and **lect**. Who has the word that describes something that is genuine and authentic?	I have the word **legible**. Who has the word that names a story or picture that uses symbolic representation?
I have the word **legitimate**. Who has the word that names what some-one of authority does if he or she says it is now within the **law** to do something?	I have the word **allegory**. Who has the word that describes what you are doing when you authorize someone else to do something for you?
I have the word **legalize**. Who has the word that names the group of people who are qualified to vote?	I have the word **delegate**. Who has the word that means to state something before there is any proof?
I have the word **electorate**. Who has the word that names a special advantage one person might be given that someone else may not have?	I have the word **allege**. Who has the word that identifies an actual **law** or group of **laws**?
I have the word **privilege**. Who has the word that names the process of voting to **choose** a winner?	I have the word **legislation**. Who has the first card?

More Greek and Latin Roots • 4–8 © 2007 Creative Teaching Press

Vocabulary Quiz: leg, lect

Shade in the bubble for the correct word.

1. Lucy felt very lucky to have been selected to participate in the talent contest. "How was Lucy feeling?"
   Ⓐ allege   Ⓑ privileged   Ⓒ electorate   Ⓓ allegory

2. Anne's cursive was improving and becoming easier to read. "Which word below means *easy to read*?"
   Ⓐ legible   Ⓑ legalize   Ⓒ delegate   Ⓓ allege

3. When you enact a law that makes an activity possible you do *this* to it.
   Ⓐ electorate   Ⓑ allegory   Ⓒ legalize   Ⓓ allege

4. The property owner said that the neighbor's dog kept getting into her backyard, but she couldn't prove how it was happening. "Which word below means accusing someone of something without proof?"
   Ⓐ legible   Ⓑ delegate   Ⓒ allege   Ⓓ legitimate

5. *The Chronicles of Narnia* are considered to be this type of literature, because each character symbolically represents something in life.
   Ⓐ allegory   Ⓑ legislation   Ⓒ delegate   Ⓓ electorate

6. When Joe was unable to attend the meeting, he authorized his coworker to submit his vote. "What is another word for *authorized*?"
   Ⓐ alleged   Ⓑ legislation   Ⓒ privilege   Ⓓ delegated

7. Mike was assured by a professional antique dealer that his vase was authentic, or *this*.
   Ⓐ legitimate   Ⓑ privilege   Ⓒ allege   Ⓓ allegory

8. Opinion polls ask a group of people about their satisfaction with the president throughout his term in office. "What is this group of people called?"
   Ⓐ electorate   Ⓑ legislation   Ⓒ legitimate   Ⓓ legible

9. The school held one of *these* to vote on which candidate they would like as class president.
   Ⓐ election   Ⓑ privilege   Ⓒ allegory   Ⓓ legislation

10. Many laws were passed last year that affected children. "What word below refers to the making of laws?"
    Ⓐ legible   Ⓑ legislation   Ⓒ elections   Ⓓ electorate

Write the correct word on the line so that the sentence makes sense and sounds grammatically correct.

11. "The woman in the store _____ that you took her purse, Mr. Saxon."

12. I will _____ the tasks to four people so that I can get the job done faster.

13. It's quite a _____ to be the first person to ride in the new sports car!

14. *Student* is to *class* as *voter* is to _____.

15. *Illegal* is to *legal* as *illegible* is to _____.

More Greek and Latin Roots • 4–8 © 2007 Creative Teaching Press

Word List: ord = order

Vocabulary	Definitions
coordinate (v)	to work together; to place in the same **order**, rank, or class
disorder (n)	confusion; disarray; lack of regular **order** or arrangement
inordinate (adj)	not regulated; **disorderly**; exceeding reasonable limits
insubordinate (adj)	not submissive to authority; does not follow **orders**
ordain (v)	to authorize; to decree or enact; to **order** by virtue of superior authority, often in religious sectors
orderly (adj)	adheres to a system; neat; systematically arranged
ordinal (adj)	being of a specified position or **order** in a numbered series
ordinance (n)	an authoritative command or **order**
subordinate (adj)	belonging to a lower rank or class; subject to the authority or control of another person; has to follow **orders**
uncoordinated (adj)	lacking planning, method, or organization

Vocabulary Sort: ord

ordinal	subordinate	uncoordinated	disorder	inordinate
ordain	orderly	insubordinate	coordinate	ordinance

to work together; to place in the same **order**, rank, or class	belonging to a lower rank or class; subject to the authority or control of another person; has to follow **orders**
adheres to a system; neat; systematically arranged	not regulated; **disorderly**; exceeding reasonable limits
not submissive to authority; does not follow **orders**	an authoritative command or **order**
confusion; disarray; lack of regular **order** or arrangement	to authorize; to decree or enact; to **order** by virtue of superior authority, often in religious sectors
lacking planning, method, or organization	being of a specified position or **order** in a numbered series

More Greek and Latin Roots • 4–8 © 2007 Creative Teaching Press

Read-Around Review: ord

I have the first card.

Who has the root that means **order**?

I have the word **uncoordinated**.

Who has the word that identifies a state of confusion or disarray?

I have the root **ord**.

Who has the word that describes someone who does not follow **orders** of authority?

I have the word **disorder**.

Who has the word that describes something that is organized and systematic?

I have the word **insubordinate**.

Who has the word that names giving authority to someone, most commonly a member of a religious group?

I have the word **orderly**.

Who has the word that means to work together with another person in an organized manner?

I have the word **ordain**.

Who has the word that identifies a command or **order** issued by a person with authority over others?

I have the word **coordinate**.

Who has the word that describes something that is **disorderly** and beyond the reasonable limits?

I have the word **ordinance**.

Who has the word that describes something that is in a specified position, such as who is the first person in line?

I have the word **inordinate**.

Who has the word that describes a person or group that is lower in rank than another?

I have the word **ordinal**.

Who has the word that describes a lack of organization or planning?

I have the word **subordinate**.

Who has the first card?

Name _____   Date _____

Vocabulary Quiz: ord

Shade in the bubble for the correct word.

1 Lydia's uncle became *this*, so he is now an authorized minister and can lead marriage ceremonies.
Ⓐ **orderly**   Ⓑ **uncoordinated**   Ⓒ **ordinal**   Ⓓ **ordained**

2 A new code of conduct or *this* in the town required shoes to be worn in all public buildings.
Ⓐ **coordinate**   Ⓑ **orderly**   Ⓒ **ordinance**   Ⓓ **subordinate**

3 What type of number is missing in this pattern: fifth, _____, seventh?
Ⓐ **ordinal**   Ⓑ **insubordinate**   Ⓒ **coordinate**   Ⓓ **inordinate**

4 To help keep his room *this* way, Dave got shelves and cubbies to organize his belongings.
Ⓐ **inordinate**   Ⓑ **ordained**   Ⓒ **subordinate**   Ⓓ **orderly**

5 If a member of the armed forces disobeys an order given by a person in command or authority, then he or she could be forced out on the basis of *this*.
Ⓐ **inordinate**   Ⓑ **orderly**   Ⓒ **ordinance**   Ⓓ **insubordination**

6 What word below describes the scattered and random arrangement of cows Mary saw on the farm?"
Ⓐ **subordinate**   Ⓑ **inordinate**   Ⓒ **ordinance**   Ⓓ **ordained**

7 What word below describes the look of a room with clothes and books all over the floor?
Ⓐ **disorder**   Ⓑ **uncoordinated**   Ⓒ **subordinate**   Ⓓ **ordinance**

8 In order for the group to get the task completed more efficiently, they will need to do *this*.
Ⓐ **inordinate**   Ⓑ **subordinate**   Ⓒ **ordained**   Ⓓ **coordinate**

9 Respectful children and young adults will treat their elders as if they are of higher rank or status. "This is because, compared to the elders, the children are considered what?"
Ⓐ **orderly**   Ⓑ **ordained**   Ⓒ **subordinate**   Ⓓ **inordinate**

10 The team lost the game because they were *this* and didn't have any method of organization.
Ⓐ **insubordinate**   Ⓑ **uncoordinated**   Ⓒ **ordinal**   Ⓓ **ordained**

Write the correct word on the line so that the sentence makes sense and sounds grammatically correct.

11 The principal had to _____ the visitation of teachers from five different schools.

12 The _____ of the small country prohibited visitors from chewing gum in public.

13 The vacation plans were so _____ that they were lucky to even find a hotel that was available upon their arrival.

14 Pope John Paul II was _____ a priest in 1946.

15 *Order* is to _____ as *organization* is to *disorganization*.

More Greek and Latin Roots • 4–8 © 2007 Creative Teaching Press

Name _____   Date _____

Review Test: leg, lect, ord

Write the correct word from the word bank to complete each sentence.

1 The committee has the authority to _____ any of
   its responsibilities to one or more subcommittees.

2 The _____ minister had the authority to perform
   the marriage ceremony.

3 Believe it or not, there is a small seaside town that has the unusual
   _____ of requiring a permit to wear certain high
   heel shoes.

4 Parables and fables are often _____ in nature so
   that the reader makes personal connections.

5 The man was defending himself against _____
   that he was speeding more than 20 miles over the limit.

6 After recess the class entered the building in such an _____
   fashion that there was no pushing or shoving.

7 Many parents signed the petition in the effort to _____
   carrying an asthma inhaler in a backpack with a doctor's authorization.

8 In college, students want to learn. Therefore, there is rarely any act of
   _____. Those students would be expelled quickly for disturbing the rights
   of other students.

9 People were upset at how _____ the state agencies appeared to be when
   faced with the natural disaster.

10 The _____ branch of government is responsible for making the laws of the country.

11 Because of the cast on her right arm, her writing was suddenly not _____.

12 When managing a team of people within any company, it is important for the boss to show respect to his
    or her _____.

13 "What a _____ it has been to see your presentation. Not everyone is given
    this opportunity."

14 A riot is an example of mass public _____, which often requires the
    involvement of the authorities.

15 In an effort to gain more votes, the candidates increased their television ad time as the _____
    day neared.

allegations
allegorical
coordinate
delegate
disorder
election
electorate
inordinate
insubordination
legalize
legible
legislative
legitimate
ordained
orderly
ordinal
ordinance
privilege
subordinates
uncoordinated

More Greek and Latin Roots • 4–8 © 2007 Creative Teaching Press

Word List: men, min, mon = to think, remind, advise, warn

Vocabulary	Definitions
admonish (v)	to **remind** of something that was forgotten or disregarded, such as an obligation or responsibility; to caution
demonstrate (v)	to show clearly and deliberately; to **advise** of how things work
menace (n)	a possible danger or threat; something or someone to **warn** others about
mention (v)	to refer to; to state in passing; to briefly or casually speak; to **remind**
monitor (n)	one who **reminds** or **advises**, especially when related to conduct
omen (n)	a sign of something about to happen; a **warning**
premonition (n)	a **warning** in advance; a **forewarning**; a feeling of evil to come
recommendation (n)	an **advised** course of action
remind (v)	to state again; to cause to remember
summon (v)	to call together to **advise**; to request to appear

For next week:
Math test
History paper
Art project

More Greek and Latin Roots • 4–8 © 2007 Creative Teaching Press

Vocabulary Sort: men, min, mon

summon	monitor	mention	demonstrate	menace
remind	recommendation	premonition	omen	admonish

a possible danger or threat; something or someone to **warn** others about	to call together to **advise**; to request to appear
a sign of something about to happen; a **warning**	to show clearly and deliberately; to **advise** of how things work
to **remind** of something that was forgotten or disregarded, such as an obligation or responsibility; to caution	to state again; to cause to remember
to refer to; to state in passing; to briefly or casually speak; to **remind**	a **warning** in advance; a **forewarning**; a feeling of evil to come
an **advised** course of action	one who **reminds** or **advises**, especially when related to conduct

Read-Around Review: men, min, mon

I have the first card.

Who has the roots that mean
to think, **remind**, **advise**, or **warn**?

I have the word **admonish**.

Who has the word that identifies what
people do when they request another
person to appear in a certain location?

I have the roots **men**, **min**, and **mon**.

Who has the word that identifies
something that is a possible danger, often
used to label a threat to society?

I have the word **summon**.

Who has the word that identifies
a person whose primary role is to **remind**
or **warn** someone of correct behavior?

I have the word **menace**.

Who has the word that means to throw a
brief comment into a conversation?

I have the word **monitor.**

Who has the word that means
a feeling ahead of time that something
is about to happen?

I have the word **mention**.

Who has the word that describes
being **advised** to do something, such as
go to a specific restaurant?

I have the word **premonition**.

Who has the word that describes
what people do when they clearly show
how something works?

I have the word **recommendation**.

Who has the word that describes
mentioning something again in order to
help someone else remember?

I have the word **demonstrate**.

Who has the word that identifies a
warning or sign of something to come?

I have the word **remind**.

Who has the word that describes what
people do when they **remind** someone
when they forgot an obligation?

I have the word **omen**.

Who has the first card?

More Greek and Latin Roots • 4–8 © 2007 Creative Teaching Press

Name _____   Date _____

Vocabulary Quiz: men, min, mon

Shade in the bubble for the correct word.

1 At a county fair, *these* are often used to show how new household gadgets work.
    Ⓐ **demonstrations**   Ⓑ **reminders**   Ⓒ **monitors**   Ⓓ **menaces**

2 Rats are often viewed as *this* because they can be a transporter of illness.
    Ⓐ **premonition**   Ⓑ **menace**   Ⓒ **monitors**   Ⓓ **summons**

3 Gerald always forgot to brush his teeth, so he needed to be *this*.
    Ⓐ **monitor**   Ⓑ **admonish**   Ⓒ **reminded**   Ⓓ **recommendation**

4 Larry had a strange feeling, or *this*, that something just wasn't right. Later, he found out that he had a rare disease.
    Ⓐ **summon**   Ⓑ **premonition**   Ⓒ **menace**   Ⓓ **recommendation**

5 When everyone at the company began leaving, she realized it was a sign that the company was having financial problems. "What is another word for this sign?"
    Ⓐ **omen**   Ⓑ **remind**   Ⓒ **summon**   Ⓓ **admonish**

6 The president of the committee did *this* when he called the members together for an emergency meeting.
    Ⓐ **premonition**   Ⓑ **summoned**   Ⓒ **monitor**   Ⓓ **demonstrated**

7 The hotel guests were were given a suggestion, or *this*, to try the local restaurant called Hurley's.
    Ⓐ **recommendation**   Ⓑ **premonition**   Ⓒ **mention**   Ⓓ **summon**

8 Lori was cautioned that if her homework wasn't completed and submitted on time for the rest of the term, then her grades would go down. "What is another word for *cautioned*?"
    Ⓐ **omen**   Ⓑ **admonished**   Ⓒ **premonition**   Ⓓ **summoned**

9 Carlos briefly stated that the rain was due to stop. "How did Carlos share this information?"
    Ⓐ **monitored**   Ⓑ **premonition**   Ⓒ **mentioned**   Ⓓ **admonished**

10 The bank manager had to do *this* with his tellers to be sure they counted the money correctly.
    Ⓐ **monitor**   Ⓑ **menace**   Ⓒ **remind**   Ⓓ **recommendation**

Write the correct word on the line so that the sentence makes sense and sounds grammatically correct.

11 Since the conversation was becoming heated, Sarah decided not to _____ her differing opinion.

12 Some people believe that if a butterfly crosses your path, it is a good _____.

13 Villains in some movies are referred to as _____ because of the havoc they create.

14 Sydney _____ how to play hopscotch to her younger brother.

15 Lucy was always forgetting to take her backpack to school, so her mom left her a note on the front door to _____ her.

More Greek and Latin Roots • 4–8 © 2007 Creative Teaching Press

Word List: cred, fid = believe, trust

Vocabulary	Definitions
affidavit (n)	a written declaration made under oath that what is stated is true; a declaration you can **trust**
bona fide (adj)	true; genuine; authentic
confidant (n)	a person who is **trusted** with secrets or private matters
confide (v)	to tell in **trust**; to disclose private matters
confident (adj)	self-assured; **belief** in oneself
credence (n)	**trustworthiness**; **belief**; acceptance as true or valid
diffident (adj)	shy and timid; reserved in manner; lacking self-confidence; not **believing** in oneself
fidelity (n)	faithfulness to obligations, duties, or observances
incredulous (adj)	unwilling or unable to **believe** something; skeptical
miscreant (n)	a **disbeliever**; an evildoer; a villain

More Greek and Latin Roots • 4–8 © 2007 Creative Teaching Press

Vocabulary Sort: cred, fid

credence	confide	fidelity	affidavit	miscreant
incredulous	diffident	confidant	confident	bona fide

true; genuine; authentic	a **disbeliever**; an evildoer; a villain
shy and timid; reserved in manner; lacking self-confidence; not **believing** in oneself	a person who is **trusted** with secrets or private matters
a written declaration made under oath that what is stated is true; a declaration you can **trust**	faithfulness to obligations, duties, or observances
unwilling or unable to **believe** something; skeptical	to tell in **trust**; to disclose private matters
self-assured; **belief** in oneself	**trustworthiness**; **belief**; acceptance as true or valid

More Greek and Latin Roots • 4–8 © 2007 Creative Teaching Press

Read-Around Review: cred, fid

I have the first card. Who has the roots that mean **believe** and **trust**?	I have the word **credence**. Who has the words that identifies something that is genuine or authentic, such as an old painting or piece of art?
I have the roots **cred** and **fid**. Who has the word that names what people do when they **entrust** their secrets to another person?	I have the words **bona fide**. Who has the word that identifies a piece of paper that proves what someone is saying is truthful?
I have the word **confide**. Who has the word that describes a person who doubts everything he or she hears?	I have the word **affidavit**. Who has the word that identifies a person to whom secret information is told and **entrusted**?
I have the word **incredulous**. Who has the word that describes a person who feels good about himself or herself?	I have the word **confidant**. Who has the word that identifies faithfulness to the duties to which one has agreed?
I have the word **confident**. Who has the word that identifies a **disbeliever** who is usually also a villain?	I have the word **fidelity**. Who has the word that describes a person who has low self-esteem and often appears to be shy?
I have the word **miscreant**. Who has the word that identifies **trustworthiness** or **belief**?	I have the word **diffident**. Who has the first card?

Name _____   Date _____

Vocabulary Quiz: cred, fid

Shade in the bubble for the correct word.

1 The leader in any organization will need to have the trustworthiness of the other members, associates, or employees to continue being successful and having *this*.

    Ⓐ **bona fide**   Ⓑ **incredulous**   Ⓒ **credence**   Ⓓ **confident**

2 The paleontologist searched for many years to find genuine dinosaur bones. "What is another word for *genuine*?"

    Ⓐ **miscreant**   Ⓑ **bona fide**   Ⓒ **diffident**   Ⓓ **affidavit**

3 Raya promised not to tell anyone about the secret plans for the invention. "What word below describes Raya?"

    Ⓐ **confidant**   Ⓑ **affidavit**   Ⓒ **miscreant**   Ⓓ **bona fide**

4 Jim was shy and had a hard time speaking in front of an audience. "What word below describes Jim?"

    Ⓐ **diffident**   Ⓑ **confidant**   Ⓒ **confided**   Ⓓ **fidelity**

5 Lucy signed *this* paper stating she would assume 25% of the costs of the home.

    Ⓐ **credence**   Ⓑ **diffident**   Ⓒ **confidant**   Ⓓ **affidavit**

6 Which word below is often incorporated into bank commercials to hint at their trustworthiness?

    Ⓐ **fidelity**   Ⓑ **incredulous**   Ⓒ **diffident**   Ⓓ **confidant**

7 Naomi's friends described her as *this* because she was skeptical of everything she heard.

    Ⓐ **credence**   Ⓑ **confidant**   Ⓒ **incredulous**   Ⓓ **affidavit**

8 A person who has friends with whom he or she can do *this* with secrets is a very lucky person.

    Ⓐ **confide**   Ⓑ **incredulous**   Ⓒ **miscreant**   Ⓓ **confident**

9 The evil warlock could not behave, so he was banished from the kingdom. "What word describes this menace?"

    Ⓐ **confidant**   Ⓑ **diffident**   Ⓒ **affidavit**   Ⓓ **miscreant**

10 Kenzie is this type of person, so she dances comfortably in front of crowds whenever possible.

    Ⓐ **confident**   Ⓑ **diffident**   Ⓒ **confidant**   Ⓓ **bona fide**

Write the correct word on the line so that the sentence makes sense and sounds grammatically correct.

11 I'm so _____ that my proposal to go to school abroad will be accepted that I've already applied for my passport.

12 A person to whom you can _____ your secrets is called your _____.

13 The boys' story about being late to school had _____ until they started talking about flying monkeys.

14 *Faithful* is to *unfaithful* as _____ is to *infidelity*.

15 *Inexpensive* is to *costly* as *fake* is to _____.

Review Test: men, min, mon, cred, fid

Write the correct word from the word bank to complete each sentence.

1 Teri was new in town and wanted to eat at a Mexican restaurant, so she asked for a _____ from her neighbor.

2 Max has such a trusting relationship with his parents that he knows he can _____ in them any secret.

3 "Oh, and I forgot to _____ that you'll be given an extra week of vacation if we meet our goals."

4 The scientist wanted to _____ the benefits of his new heart monitor to the medical industry.

5 As a young child, Jordan was _____ and quiet. However, as she grew older, she became more confident and outgoing.

6 The owners of the vineyard hired a _____ to observe the workers' speed and precision during the grape harvest season.

7 "I'm sure that there's no need to _____ you of the date of my birthday," said Lisa.

8 Megan wanted to have a meeting, so she _____ all of the members of her cheerleading squad.

9 All construction came to a complete halt when some workers discovered a _____ Native American skull at the ancient burial site.

10 California is the last state that still prohibits ferret species as pets, because many farmers still view them as _____.

11 When she was faced with a difficult decision, she knew to call her _____. That was the only person she trusted with her deepest secrets.

12 Some people believe that if a black cat crosses your path, it is a bad _____.

13 One of the promises made in a marriage agreement is _____, as both partners promise to remain faithful to each other.

14 After completing the exam, Seth signed an _____ stating that he did not cheat in any way.

15 A person with a higher tolerance for risk in life usually has a more _____ personality than someone who is afraid to try new things.

Word Bank

admonish
affidavit
bona fide
confidant
confide
confident
credence
demonstrate
diffident
fidelity
incredulous
menaces
mention
miscreant
monitor
omen
premonition
recommendation
remind
summoned

More Greek and Latin Roots • 4–8 © 2007 Creative Teaching Press

Word List: pass, path, pat = feeling, emotion, suffering

Vocabulary	Definitions
apathy (n)	lack of interest or concern; lack of **emotion** or **feeling**
compassion (n)	deep **feeling** or awareness of the **suffering** of another accompanied with the desire to relieve the **suffering**
compatible (adj)	able to get along; agreeable
dispassionate (adj)	unaffected by **emotion** or bias
empathy (n)	understanding of another person's **feelings** or situation
passionate (adj)	having or showing strong **emotion**
pathetic (adj)	capable of making one **feel** sympathetic or compassionate
pathos (n)	the **feeling** of pity or sympathy
patient (adj)	able to wait; bearing pains or trials calmly and without complaint; calm
sympathetic (adj)	expressing **feelings** of sorrow or pity for someone else

More Greek and Latin Roots • 4–8 © 2007 Creative Teaching Press

Vocabulary Sort: pass, path, pat

pathetic	apathy	compatible	sympathetic	pathos
patient	dispassionate	compassion	empathy	passionate

lack of interest or concern; lack of **emotion** or **feeling**	expressing **feelings** of sorrow or pity for someone else
the **feeling** of pity or sympathy	deep **feeling** or awareness of the **suffering** of another accompanied with the desire to relieve the **suffering**
able to get along; agreeable	having or showing strong **emotion**
understanding of another person's **feelings** or situation	unaffected by **emotion** or bias
capable of making one **feel** sympathetic or compassionate	able to wait; bearing pains or trials calmly and without complaint; calm

More Greek and Latin Roots • 4–8 © 2007 Creative Teaching Press

Read-Around Review: pass, path, pat

I have the first card. Who has the roots that mean **feeling**, **emotion**, and **suffering**?	I have the word **dispassionate**. Who has the word that describes people who can usually get along because they share similar **feelings** or interests?
I have the roots **pass**, **path**, and **pat**. Who has the word that describes when a person identifies with and understands another person's **feelings**?	I have the word **compatible**. Who has the word that identifies an overall lack of interest or **feeling**?
I have the word **empathy**. Who has the word that names the deep awareness of the **suffering** of others and a desire to help?	I have the word **apathy**. Who has the word that describes something that makes a person **feel** pity, often with some negative **feelings** attached?
I have the word **compassion**. Who has the word that describes a person who can wait calmly, even when in pain, without complaining?	I have the word **pathetic**. Who has the word that describes a person who displays strong **emotion** about a topic?
I have the word **patient**. Who has the word that identifies a general **feeling** of sadness, pity, or sympathy, such as when one **feels** "down"?	I have the word **passionate**. Who has the word that describes what you **feel** towards the family at a funeral?
I have the word **pathos**. Who has the word that describes someone who is not affected by **emotion**, enabling the person to be fair and unbiased?	I have the word **sympathetic**. Who has the first card?

More Greek and Latin Roots • 4–8 © 2007 Creative Teaching Press

Vocabulary Quiz: pass, path, pat

Shade in the bubble for the correct word.

1 People who feel badly for mistreated animals have *this*, and are often motivated to volunteer at shelters.
Ⓐ **apathy**   Ⓑ **empathy**   Ⓒ **pathos**   Ⓓ **compassion**

2 Which word below describes the emotionally charged crowd that began to yell in protest to a decision?
Ⓐ **passionate**   Ⓑ **empathy**   Ⓒ **sympathy**   Ⓓ **compassion**

3 Which word below describes someone that understands how other people feel?
Ⓐ **pathetic**   Ⓑ **empathetic**   Ⓒ **pathos**   Ⓓ **compatible**

4 The family was shocked at the lack of concern shown by the town when their house burned down. "What word below describes the town's behavior?"
Ⓐ **apathetic**   Ⓑ **pathetic**   Ⓒ **empathy**   Ⓓ **sympathy**

5 The Olsen family was *this* as they waited nearly two years for the remodeling of the house to be finished.
Ⓐ **patient**   Ⓑ **sympathetic**   Ⓒ **passionate**   Ⓓ **apathy**

6 Pete showed signs of concern for his injured friend. "What word below describes how Pete felt?"
Ⓐ **pathetic**   Ⓑ **passionate**   Ⓒ **apathy**   Ⓓ **sympathetic**

7 Francisco was feeling sorry for himself, but he didn't want to do anything to improve his situation. "What word below identifies Francisco's feelings?"
Ⓐ **compassion**   Ⓑ **passionate**   Ⓒ **pathos**   Ⓓ **compatible**

8 Publicly elected officials need to be *this* so people will trust in their ability to make fair judgments.
Ⓐ **empathy**   Ⓑ **dispassionate**   Ⓒ **pathetic**   Ⓓ **pathos**

9 Roommates need to be *this* so they can get along with each other.
Ⓐ **empathy**   Ⓑ **passionate**   Ⓒ **compatible**   Ⓓ **sympathy**

10 The building was in such pitiful or *this* condition that it sold for thousands less than it was worth.
Ⓐ **pathetic**   Ⓑ **sympathy**   Ⓒ **patient**   Ⓓ **dispassionate**

Write the correct word on the line so that the sentence makes sense and sounds grammatically correct.

11 When driving on the road in a crowded city, it's important to be a _____ driver.

12 Jill bought a hybrid car because she was _____ about the environment.

13 Teachers love it when they have a classroom of students who are all _____ with each other.

14 A jury needs to be _____ when hearing a case in a courtroom. Otherwise, someone could be punished for something he or she didn't even do.

15 *Cruel* is to _____ as *menacing* is to *helpful*.

136

Word List: dur, firm = to harden, hold out, last, make firm, strengthen

Vocabulary	Definitions
affirm (v)	to support or **uphold** the validity of; to maintain as true
affirmative (adj)	describes a reply of "yes"; positive; optimistic; asserting that something is true
confirm (v)	to **strengthen**; to support or establish the certainty of something; validate
confirmation (n)	verification; additional proof that something is correct
durable (adj)	sturdy; able to **hold up** for a long period of time; **lasting**
duration (n)	a period of time; a **lasting** period
duress (n)	being **held** or constrained by threat; coerced; forcible confinement
endurance (n)	the power to withstand or **hold up** to stress or hardship
endure (v)	able to **last**; tolerate
indurate (adj)	emotionally **hardened**; callous indifference; fixed or established in thoughts

SUMMIT 6miles

Vocabulary Sort: dur, firm

endurance	affirm	confirm	indurate	endure
duration	durable	affirmative	confirmation	duress

a period of time; a **lasting** period	able to **last**; tolerate
to **strengthen**; to support or establish the certainty of something; validate	describes a reply of "yes"; positive; optimistic; asserting that something is true
the power to withstand or **hold up** to stress or hardship	being **held** or constrained by threat; coerced; forcible confinement
emotionally **hardened**; callous indifference; fixed or established in thoughts	verification; additional proof that something is correct
to support or **uphold** the validity of; to maintain as true	sturdy; able to **hold up** for a long period of time; **lasting**

More Greek and Latin Roots • 4–8 © 2007 Creative Teaching Press

Read-Around Review: dur, firm

I have the first card.

Who has the roots that mean
to harden, **hold out**, **last**, **make firm**,
and **strengthen**?

I have the roots **dur** and **firm**.

Who has the word that names
what people do when they tolerate
something for a long period of time?

I have the word **endure**.

Who has the word that identifies
verification that something is correct, and
which is usually submitted in writing?

I have the word **confirmation**.

Who has the word that describes
a person who has become emotionally
hard and inflexible?

I have the word **indurate**.

Who has the word that identifies
a length of time?

I have the word **duration**.

Who has the word that identifies
what people do when they validate
the truth of something?

I have the word **confirm**.

Who has the word that describes
anything that is sturdy and able to
withstand wear and tear?

I have the word **durable**.

Who has the word that labels
how a person might be **held** against
his or her will?

I have the word **duress**.

Who has the word that describes a
positive reply of "yes," especially in a vote?

I have the word **affirmative**.

Who has the word that names what a
person needs in order to run a marathon
or **last** for a long time without pain?

I have the word **endurance**.

Who has the word that means to
support or maintain as true?

I have the word **affirm**.

Who has the first card?

Name _____ Date _____

Vocabulary Quiz: dur, firm

Shade in the bubble for the correct word.

1. The Marine sergeant used this word to show he agreed with the decision made by his commander.
   Ⓐ durable Ⓑ duress Ⓒ indurate Ⓓ affirmative

2. After buying shares of the company, Sue received this type of letter stating that she owned part of it.
   Ⓐ confirmation Ⓑ duration Ⓒ endurance Ⓓ indurate

3. The first denim jeans were designed by Levi Strauss to withstand a great deal of hard work by the miners during the Gold Rush in California. "What word below describes the jeans?"
   Ⓐ duress Ⓑ durable Ⓒ indurate Ⓓ confirm

4. Spending six years in youth hostels while traveling through Europe made Paul self-reliant and hardened. "What word below describes Paul?"
   Ⓐ indurate Ⓑ affirmed Ⓒ affirmative Ⓓ confirmation

5. After buying something on the Internet, a company will send an e-mail to the buyer to do *this*, stating that they did receive the order.
   Ⓐ confirm Ⓑ affirm Ⓒ endure Ⓓ duress

6. Spending three weeks in the hospital was not what Ellen had planned on doing during her summer vacation. "What word below describes that length of time?"
   Ⓐ duration Ⓑ confirmation Ⓒ indurate Ⓓ affirming

7. Maria would need *this* to withstand the harsh temperatures and high altitude in the Swiss Alps.
   Ⓐ affirmative Ⓑ endurance Ⓒ duress Ⓓ confirmation

8. Which word below describes the years of suffering Sam experienced while being held captive deep in the jungles of Africa?
   Ⓐ affirmed Ⓑ duress Ⓒ confirmed Ⓓ affirmation

9. Which word below describes the action of believing that what someone has stated is the complete truth?
   Ⓐ indurate Ⓑ endure Ⓒ affirm Ⓓ duration

10. A famous magician lasted 44 days in a clear box without any food. "What is another word for *lasted*?"
    Ⓐ affirmation Ⓑ duress Ⓒ confirmation Ⓓ endured

Write the correct word on the line so that the sentence makes sense and sounds grammatically correct.

11. The biologist photographed the chimps throughout the _____ of her stay in the jungle.

12. Participating in any lengthy athletic competition requires a great deal of _____.

13. Max received his _____ stating that he had registered for the Grilling Party.

14. *Weak* is to *strong* as *flimsy* is to _____.

15. *Disconfirm* is to *confirm* as *disaffirm* is to _____.

More Greek and Latin Roots • 4–8 © 2007 Creative Teaching Press

Review Test: pass, path, pat, dur, firm

Write the correct word from the word bank to complete each sentence.

1. The newspapers and Web sites were quick to _____ that the two stars of the show did in fact get married last weekend.

2. He's afraid to travel to Hawaii, because he doesn't think he'll be able to _____ the humidity and heat.

3. Luckily, the two rabbits she rescued were _____, so they will be able to share the same habitat.

4. "I _____ that I am the person who has completed this written examination, and that I have done so fairly without any help."

5. The children were so _____ even though the server took more than 45 minutes to bring their meals. They quietly played games on napkins with each other.

6. The reporter stated that the civilians were being held under _____ in an unknown location of the war-torn country.

7. The young man told the speaker that he had _____ for him because he was treated the same way as a child.

8. Matthew was so _____ about helping homeless animals that he organized a bake sale to raise money for the animal shelter.

9. The mourners at the funeral were _____ to the feelings of the family members.

10. There seems to be _____ among many people who don't appear to care that there are many homeless people living on the streets.

11. It is estimated that the _____ of the entire test will be one hour.

12. Cars, appliances, equipment, and home furnishings are examples of _____ goods purchased by consumers to last many years.

13. The singer had incredible vocal _____ to be able to sing for three straight hours to the crowd of thousands.

14. Due to her deep _____ for people, Linda organized fund-raisers to earn money for local shelters.

15. A mediator is a person who tries to help people in the middle of a disagreement. The role requires the person to be _____, so that one side does not get treated any differently from the other.

Word Bank
affirm
affirmative
apathy
compassion
compatible
confirm
confirmation
dispassionate
durable
duration
duress
empathy
endurance
endure
indurate
passionate
pathetic
pathos
patient
sympathetic

More Greek and Latin Roots • 4–8 © 2007 Creative Teaching Press

Answer Key

Page 10
1. B
2. A
3. A
4. D
5. C
6. A
7. D
8. A
9. D
10. C
11. promotions
12. mobilize
13. motivation
14. removed
15. demoted

Page 14
1. A
2. D
3. B
4. A
5. B
6. C
7. D
8. A
9. A
10. C
11. aggressive
12. degrading
13. gradually, centigrade
14. progress
15. upgrading

Page 15
1. promote
2. progress
3. demote
4. upgrade
5. graduation
6. motivate
7. removal
8. gradual
9. aggression
10. mobility
11. digressing
12. regressed
13. degraded
14. mobilize
15. progression

Page 19
1. C
2. B
3. A
4. D
5. A
6. A
7. B
8. D
9. A
10. A
11. imposition
12. exposed
13. post
14. proposal
15. compose

Page 23
1. B
2. A
3. D
4. A
5. D
6. A
7. D
8. B
9. C
10. A
11. residence
12. session
13. sedative
14. sediment
15. sedentary

Page 24
1. deposit
2. sedan
3. session
4. expose
5. imposition
6. sediment
7. posted
8. sedate
9. composing
10. proposal
11. sedentary
12. juxtapose
13. reside
14. transposed
15. residence

Page 28
1. A
2. D
3. A
4. D
5. A
6. A
7. D
8. A
9. D
10. A
11. dialog
12. logo
13. analogy
14. prologue
15. eulogy

Page 32
1. D
2. D
3. B
4. A
5. A
6. A
7. D
8. D
9. A
10. B
11. antonyms
12. homonyms
13. acronyms
14. oronym
15. synonyms

Page 33
1. logbook
2. acronyms
3. anonymous
4. eulogy
5. onomatopoeia
6. logo
7. antonyms
8. synonym
9. eponym
10. apology
11. pseudonym
12. logical
13. epilogue
14. homonyms
15. prologue

Page 37
1. C
2. A
3. B
4. C
5. A
6. C
7. D
8. A
9. D
10. A
11. extend
12. contain
13. abstain
14. detained
15. tentative

Page 41
1. A
2. D
3. C
4. A
5. D
6. D
7. B
8. A
9. B
10. C
11. differed
12. fertile
13. infer
14. prefer
15. transfer

Page 42
1. extend
2. differ
3. circumference
4. tenant
5. detained
6. infer
7. offering
8. prefer
9. referral
10. transfer
11. tentative
12. patent
13. chauffeur
14. conference
15. contains

Page 46
1. A
2. A
3. D
4. A
5. B
6. A
7. C
8. B
9. A
10. D
11. caption
12. encapsulate
13. capitalize
14. capacity
15. capture

Page 50
1. A
2. D
3. B
4. B
5. A
6. A
7. D
8. B
9. B
10. A
11. repulsive
12. pulsating
13. dispel
14. repellent
15. impulse

Page 51
1. captioned
2. capsized
3. pulsating
4. compelled
5. expel
6. capacity
7. capitalize
8. capture
9. propel
10. impulse
11. repellent
12. repulsive
13. capable
14. recapitulation
15. encapsulate

Answer Key

Page 55
1. B
2. A
3. B
4. A
5. A
6. A
7. A
8. D
9. C
10. B
11. impending
12. pending
13. pendulum
14. expenditures
15. dependent

Page 59
1. D
2. A
3. A
4. B
5. D
6. A
7. B
8. A
9. C
10. A
11. station
12. status
13. estate
14. ecstatic
15. status quo

Page 60
1. pendant
2. thermostat
3. expenditures
4. impending
5. independent
6. pending
7. statutes
8. stationary
9. dependent
10. ecstatic
11. estate
12. pendulum
13. suspended
14. stations
15. status quo

Page 64
1. A
2. C
3. C
4. A
5. D
6. A
7. C
8. D
9. A
10. D
11. conscience
12. recognize
13. unconscionable
14. omniscient
15. conscientious

Page 68
1. B
2. D
3. C
4. D
5. A
6. D
7. A
8. D
9. C
10. A
11. resent
12. nonsense
13. sensible
14. consensus
15. dissenter

Page 69
1. dissenter
2. sensitive
3. incognito
4. omniscient
5. conscientious
6. conscience
7. desensitize
8. consensus
9. unconscionable
10. resent
11. recognize
12. cognizant
13. nonsense
14. scientists
15. sentimental

Page 73
1. D
2. B
3. A
4. C
5. D
6. B
7. A
8. D
9. A
10. A
11. conducive
12. introduced
13. deduction
14. produce
15. deduce

Page 77
1. B
2. A
3. D
4. A
5. C
6. C
7. B
8. B
9. A
10. A
11. fluid
12. influx
13. influential
14. fluctuate
15. confluence

Page 78
1. reduce
2. fluent
3. influx
4. influential
5. fluctuates
6. introduction
7. conducive
8. deduce
9. deductible
10. produced
11. introduce
12. deductions
13. affluence
14. confluence
15. superfluous

Page 82
1. C
2. A
3. A
4. D
5. B
6. A
7. D
8. D
9. A
10. D
11. audible
12. sonnet
13. unison
14. phonograph
15. cacophonic

Page 86
1. A
2. B
3. A
4. D
5. A
6. A
7. D
8. B
9. D
10. D
11. tangent
12. contiguous
13. tangible
14. contagious
15. tactile

Page 87
1. unison
2. tangible
3. tangent
4. tangled
5. audible
6. sonnet
7. contact
8. intact
9. resonate
10. contiguous
11. cacophony
12. audio
13. tangy
14. contagious
15. auditorium

Page 91
1. B
2. A
3. D
4. A
5. D
6. C
7. A
8. D
9. B
10. D
11. exclusive
12. reclusive
13. secluded
14. conclude
15. cluster

Page 95
1. D
2. A
3. B
4. A
5. A
6. D
7. B
8. A
9. D
10. C
11. corresponding
12. responsive
13. spontaneously
14. despondent
15. responsible

Page 96
1. secluded
2. irresponsible
3. correspond
4. despondent
5. exclude
6. enclose
7. responsible
8. respond
9. claustrophobic
10. conclusion
11. exclusive
12. sponsor
13. cluster
14. spontaneous
15. responsive

Answer Key

Page 100
1. A
2. C
3. B
4. D
5. A
6. A
7. D
8. C
9. A
10. A
11. potions
12. potential
13. devalued
14. valor
15. impotent

Page 104
1. B
2. B
3. A
4. A
5. D
6. A
7. A
8. B
9. B
10. A
11. citation
12. policy
13. police
14. citadel
15. metropolis

Page 105
1. nepotism
2. impotent
3. policy
4. Citadel
5. metropolis
6. potential
7. potent
8. omnipotent
9. possessed
10. police
11. civilly
12. Valor
13. civilizations
14. citations
15. devalued

Page 109
1. B
2. A
3. A
4. B
5. D
6. A
7. A
8. D
9. B
10. A
11. affect
12. facilitate
13. factor
14. benefactor
15. effect

Page 113
1. C
2. B
3. A
4. A
5. D
6. C
7. A
8. A
9. D
10. A
11. ensemble
12. assimilate
13. simulation
14. assemble
15. simile

Page 114
1. facilitate
2. resemble
3. mimic
4. factors
5. benefactors
6. deface
7. effects
8. simulation
9. factory, manufactured
10. simultaneously
11. infect
12. ensemble
13. assemble
14. affect
15. semblance

Page 118
1. B
2. A
3. C
4. C
5. A
6. D
7. A
8. A
9. A
10. B
11. alleges
12. delegate
13. privilege
14. electorate
15. legible

Page 122
1. D
2. C
3. A
4. D
5. D
6. B
7. A
8. D
9. C
10. B
11. coordinate
12. ordinance
13. uncoordinated
14. ordained
15. disorder

Page 123
1. delegate
2. ordained
3. ordinance
4. allegorical
5. allegations
6. orderly
7. legalize
8. insubordination
9. uncoordinated
10. legislative
11. legible
12. subordinates
13. privilege
14. disorder
15. election

Page 127
1. A
2. B
3. C
4. B
5. A
6. B
7. A
8. B
9. C
10. A
11. mention
12. omen
13. menaces
14. demonstrated
15. remind

Page 131
1. C
2. B
3. A
4. A
5. D
6. A
7. C
8. A
9. D
10. A
11. confident
12. confide, confidant
13. credence
14. fidelity
15. bona fide

Page 132
1. recommendation
2. confide
3. mention
4. demonstrate
5. diffident
6. monitor
7. remind
8. summoned
9. bona fide
10. menaces
11. confidant
12. omen
13. fidelity
14. affidavit
15. confident

Page 136
1. D
2. A
3. B
4. A
5. A
6. D
7. C
8. B
9. C
10. A
11. patient
12. passionate
13. compatible
14. dispassionate
15. compassion

Page 140
1. D
2. A
3. B
4. A
5. A
6. A
7. B
8. B
9. C
10. D
11. duration
12. endurance
13. confirmation
14. durable
15. affirm

Page 141
1. confirm
2. endure
3. compatible
4. affirm
5. patient
6. duress
7. empathy
8. passionate
9. sympathetic
10. apathy
11. duration
12. durable
13. endurance
14. compassion
15. dispassionate